DISSEC[ ]
THE DIGITAL
DOLLAR

SECOND EDITION

DISSECTING THE DIGITAL DOLLAR

Published by the Music Managers Forum

Produced by CMU Insights

Written by Chris Cooke

© Music Managers Forum 2018

A big thank you to the many people who contributed insight and information to our research by taking part in our roundtable debates, completing our manager survey or agreeing to be interviewed by the author.

Thanks also to the teams at MMF and CMU Insights, and other supporters of the project, who have helped in the editing, production and promotion of the 'Dissecting The Digital Dollar' reports, including: Adam Webb, Annabella Coldrick, Amanda Harcourt, Andy Edwards, Andy Malt, Caroline Moses, Chris Carey, Cliff Fluet, Fiona McGugan, Indy Vidyalankara, James Barton, Jon Webster, Phoebe Rodwell, Sam Taylor, Sophie Goossens and Tom Frederikse.

For updates on future phases of the 'Dissecting The Digital Dollar' project follow the MMF on social media. Artist managers and music companies can also access extra research, tools and events by joining the MMF. Information on how to join is available at themmf.net

For more CMU you can sign up to the CMU Daily bulletin or Setlist podcast at cmusignup.com. For more on the training and consultancy services available from CMU Insights check cmuinsights.com

themmf.net | @mmfuk

cmuinsights.com | @cmu

DISSECTING THE DIGITAL DOLLAR

ABOUT THE MUSIC MANAGERS FORUM

MMF is the largest professional community of music managers in the world. Since our inception in 1992 we have worked hard to educate, inform and represent our managers as well as offering a network through which managers can share experiences, opportunities and information.

We are a community of 500+ managers who operate global businesses from the UK and a wider network of over 2000 managers globally. We engage, advise and lobby industry associates and provide a professional voice on wider industry issues relevant to managers and the artists they represent.

The MMF also runs training programmes, courses and events designed to educate and inform artist managers as well as regular seminars, open meetings, roundtables, discount programmes and the Artist & Manager Awards.

ABOUT CMU INSIGHTS

CMU is a service provider to the music industry best known for its various media: free daily news bulletin the CMU Daily, weekly podcast Setlist, and premium services CMU Digest and CMU Trends.

CMU Insights provides training and consultancy to music companies and companies working with music. We offer training and research services; seminars and masterclasses; and insight sessions at music conferences around the world.

ABOUT THE AUTHOR

Chris Cooke is MD and Business Editor of CMU, writing for its media, co-hosting its podcast, and leading on the CMU Insights training and consultancy projects. He also heads up the CMU:DIY education programme for young artists.

CMU is part of Chris's company 3CM UnLimited, through which he also publishes cultural recommendations service ThisWeek London and its sister magazine ThreeWeeks Edinburgh; and helps to run award winning PR training charity the Taylor Bennett Foundation.

With degrees in English and Law, Chris regularly writes about, discusses and comments on the music business, intellectual property matters, and the media and communication sectors.

INTRODUCTION

The growth of music streaming has dramatically changed the business of recorded music. Instead of sharing in the proceeds of a physical or digital sale, music makers and rights holders are now participating in new commercial models based on revenue share and micro-payments.

These new dynamics have initiated a thousand debates – is there too little money or too much information? Are we destroying music or creating a new world of opportunities for fan engagement? Artists had questions for managers. Managers had questions for record labels and music publishers. Few had conclusive answers. Not least about the industry's digital deals and how revenues are calculated, reported and shared between the music community.

As a result, back in 2014, the Music Managers Forum asked Chris Cooke of CMU Insights to research how streaming services are licensed and how the money flows. The resulting report, 'Dissecting The Digital Dollar', was published in 2015 and became an obligatory read for anyone trying to understand the digital music market.

It also threw up further topics for debate. For instance: are the splits in the new digital pie broadly fair to both performers and songwriters? Should artists receive direct payments from streaming plays similar to those from radio broadcasts? What are the implications of non-disclosure agreements? How important is metadata in ensuring the money flows correctly? And how do YouTube and other opt-out services fit into the picture?

So many questions, in fact, that the MMF decided to host a series of roundtables in 2016. These involved over 200 participants across the UK, France, USA and Canada, with labels, publishers, accountants, lawyers, songwriters, performers and, of course, managers all taking part.

In each roundtable we debated the issues, and in October that year we published Part Two of 'Dissecting The Digital Dollar', which aimed to summarise our findings as well as outlining some key recommendations for managers, the industry and regulators for what needed to change in the world of digital music.

This report has informed MMF policy positions and campaigning in the context of the European Union's new copyright directive, and assisted us in joining up with other organisations representing music makers around the common cause of fairness and transparency in the digital age.

For the MMF, we realised that part of our role is helping artists and managers navigate the opportunities and innovations that music streaming creates, and so this year we researched and produced two further guides – the 'Deals Guide' outlining the ten kinds of label/distributor deals now available to artists, and the 'Transparency Guide' identifying 20 different data types that artists and managers should demand in order to do their jobs and be assured that the remuneration received from streaming is the remuneration due.

These were accompanied by a Digital Deals Comparison Calculator that helps predict the flow and return of digital income over time, and how that income is shared between label and artist depending which of the ten deal types are employed, as well as identifying the trade offs involved in each arrangement.

This book, 'Dissecting The Digital Dollar: Second Edition', updates and combines all this work in one place. Its publication results from many conversations with people in the music industry, and with educators and students, who have asked us for a physical version.

We hope you find it valuable and we welcome ideas and input on where we should go next in our quest to better explain and truly transform the music industry.

Annabella Coldrick
Chief Executive, Music Managers Forum
January 2018

SECTION ONE:
EXECUTIVE SUMMARY

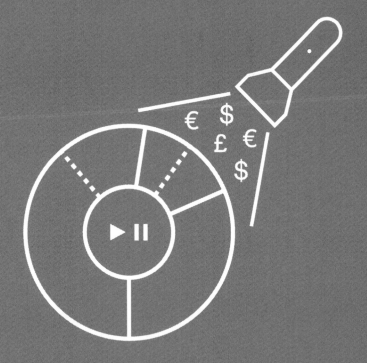

The rise of digital has created both challenges and opportunities for the music industry. The challenges around piracy have been widely documented, but working with legitimate digital services has also been challenging for music rights owners, especially as we have seen a shift from downloads to streams, because licensing these platforms requires a new approach to doing business.

Over the last decade the music rights sector has been busy evolving new licensing models and new industry standards have started to emerge. However, issues remain, and there is some debate as to whether both the fundamentals and the specifics of these new business models are the best possible solutions, and whether or not they have been created to be more beneficial to some stakeholders in the music community than others.

And even where standards are emerging, there remains much confusion in the wider music community as to how, exactly, streaming services are being licensed, how it is calculated what digital service providers (DSPs) must pay, and how that money is then processed and shared by the music rights industry.

There are various reasons for this confusion...

▶ The complicated nature of the streaming deals.

▶ The record industry and music publishing sector do not always license in the same way.

▶ The way services are licensed and royalties processed can vary from country to country.

▶ Most streaming deals are ultimately revenue share arrangements, making exact payments per usage less predictable.

▶ The specifics of many streaming deals are secret due to non-disclosure agreements in key contracts.

▶ Those who have led on the development of new licensing arrangements have often done a poor job of communicating them to other stakeholders.

In evolving these new licensing models, record companies, music publishers and collective management organisations (CMOs) have had to navigate copyright laws and other music industry conventions which were not specifically developed with the digital distribution of recorded content in mind.

In doing so, some assumptions have been made which perhaps, with hindsight, require more consideration, either by lawmakers, courts or the wider music community. Or, at least, a more unified approach across the industry, and across the world.

DISSECTING THE DIGITAL DOLLAR

In order to inform this debate, in 2015 the UK's Music Managers Forum commissioned the 'Dissecting The Digital Dollar' report, to review and explain how music rights have been exploited in the past, how digital licensing has evolved, and what issues now need to be tackled.

We spoke in depth to over 30 leading practitioners from across the music, digital and legal sectors, and surveyed 50 artist managers in five markets who, between them, represent artists signed to all three major music companies and over 100 independent labels.

Following the publication of Part One of 'Dissecting The Digital Dollar' the MMF staged a series of roundtable debates in four countries, involving artists, songwriters, labels, publishers, lawyers, accountants and artist managers, to discuss the issues raised in the report. These debates – a detailed summary of which was published by MMF in 2016 – provided an overview of the music community's views on the various issues, and identified where there was consensus and where there were disagreements. They also informed MMF's own policies and resulted in two additional guides being commissioned.

This book brings brings together an updated version of the original report, a summary of the roundtable discussions, and the two new guides.

The way music rights work varies around the world, partly because of differences in copyright law, and partly because of different practices and conventions that have evolved in each market. This variation is in itself a challenge in a digital sector where so many services aspire to be truly global.

It also poses challenges in explaining how music copyright works on a general or global level, because different rules, technicalities and terminology may apply in any one country; and there are significant differences of emphasis between so called 'common law' jurisdictions, like the UK and the US, and 'civil law' systems, like France and Spain.

Although we have tried to be 'market neutral' in describing the basics of music copyright in this book, we are arguably starting from a common law and possibly UK perspective, but we will try to be clear where the key differences exist between different systems.

MUSIC RIGHTS & DIGITAL PLATFORMS: HOW IT WORKS

1. Copyright provides creators with controls that can be exploited for profit

Copyright is ultimately about providing creators with certain controls over that which they create, either as a point of principle, and/or to encourage and enable creativity by allowing creators and their business partners to exploit these controls for profit.

Exactly what controls a copyright owner enjoys varies from country to country, but they commonly include the exclusive right to make and distribute copies of a creative work, to adapt the work, to rent it out or communicate it, and to perform it in public.

Copyright makes money when third parties wish to exploit one of these controls, because the third party must get permission – ie a 'licence' – from the copyright owner. The licensor will usually charge the licensee a fee to grant permission.

2. The core music rights

The music industry controls and exploits various kinds of intellectual property, though the core music rights are the separate copyrights in songs (lyrics and composition) and sound recordings, what civil law systems might refer to as the separate 'author rights' and 'neighbouring' rights.

Both copyright law and the music industry routinely treat these two kinds of copyright differently. Within the business, music publishers (and their CMOs) generally control song copyrights while record companies control recording rights.

This is important for anyone wishing to license a recording of a song, because it means they will need to do separate deals with both record companies and music publishers, and the labels and publishers may have different ways of doing the deal.

3. The licensing process will differ depending on usage

How labels and publishers go about licensing any one licensee will often depend on which of the aforementioned 'controls' said licensee wishes to exploit.

For example, if they wish to exploit the reproduction and distribution controls – what might be called the 'reproduction' or 'mechanical rights' – they may be licensed in a different way than if they wish to exploit the performance or communication controls – what might be called the 'performing' or 'neighbouring rights' (this being a different use of the term 'neighbouring rights').

Sometimes rights owners license 'collectively', as opposed to individual rights owners and licensees having a direct relationship. When this happens all labels or all publishers appoint a collective management organisation to license on their behalf.

This may be done for practical reasons, or because copyright law instigates a 'compulsory license', meaning that a rights owner cannot refuse to license in a certain scenario, even though licensees are still obliged to pay royalties. Collective licensing is usually subject to extra regulation with a statutory body or court possibly empowered to ultimately set royalty rates.

WHICH COPYRIGHTS AND CONTROLS?

You burn a copy of a track onto CD

You are exploiting the 'reproduction control' of both the song and recording copyright

(what music publishers call the 'mechanical rights')

You perform a song at a gig

You are exploiting the 'public performance control' of just the song copyright

You play a track on the radio

You are exploiting the 'communication control' of both the song and recording copyright

You synchronise a track to a TV show

You are exploiting the 'reproduction control' of both the song and recording copyright when you actually synchronise the track...

and then the 'communication control' of both the song and recording copyright when the TV show is broadcast

You download or stream a track

You are exploiting both the 'reproduction control' and the 'communication control'* (possibly the specific 'making available control') of both the song and recording copyright

*This can vary from country to country, for example in the US only a reproduction rights licence is required for downloads, while only a performing rights licence is required for personalised radio services.

In the main (there are exceptions, for example in TV sync), labels commonly license reproduction rights directly but performing rights collectively, whereas publishers often license both sets of rights through their CMOs, but possibly different CMOs (in the UK, MCPS and PRS respectively).

4. It is important to know who controls each copyright

Unlike other kinds of intellectual property, copyright is not usually registered with a statutory authority, which can make identifying owners tricky.

Copyright law usually defines 'default' or 'presumed' owners of new works, though these rules vary from country to country, and can be different for songs and recordings. Default owners can also usually transfer ownership, or at least control, to another party – usually in return for money – through so called 'assignment' or 'licensing' agreements.

As a result, whatever default ownership rules may say, most songs are either owned or at least controlled by music publishers, and most recordings are either owned or at least controlled by record companies. Singer songwriters, involved in creating both songs and recordings, will usually have separate deals with separate companies covering their respective song and recording rights.

Though there is an important distinction to make when it comes to songs, in that a songwriter will commonly directly appoint a CMO to control some elements of their copyright and a music publisher to control the other elements. So in the UK, a songwriter assigns performing rights to PRS but all the other rights to their publisher. The publisher then has a contractual right to share in performing rights revenue, but does not actually control that element of the copyright.

Finally, copyrights can be co-owned. This is particularly common with song copyrights, because collaboration is common in songwriting. Where a song is co-owned, a licensee will usually need permission from each and every stakeholder to make use of the work.

5. Creator & Performer Rights

Artists and songwriters often assign – or as good as – the copyright in their recordings and songs to record labels and music publishers; this is especially true with new talent who need their corporate partners to make risky investments in their careers in the form of artistic development, content production, marketing and cash advances.

But artists and songwriters will still retain some rights in relation to those recordings and songs through their record and publishing contracts. In particular the right to share in any revenue generated by their work, and maybe also rights to consultation, approval or veto in relation to certain uses of their work.

In addition to these contractual rights, artists and songwriters may

WHO CONTROLS THE MUSIC RIGHTS?

A label sends artists into the studio to write and record new music ... a song and a recording is created

SONG COPYRIGHT

WHO OWNS THIS? By default, usually the songwriter or songwriters, though they will often transfer ownership and/or control to other parties.

WHAT RIGHTS? The copyright provides a number of 'controls'. The songwriter commonly transfers some controls to a 'collective management organisation' and the other controls to a publisher. In the UK: 'performing rights' to CMO, other rights to the publisher.

PERFORMING RIGHTS OF THE SONG COPYRIGHT	OTHER ELEMENTS OF THE SONG COPYRIGHT
CMO (PRS in the UK)	MUSIC PUBLISHER
CMO handles licensing	Publisher either licenses direct or via a CMO (MCPS in UK)
CMO passes 50% of income to publisher and 50% to songwriter	Publisher pays royalty to songwriter according to publishing contract

RECORDING COPYRIGHT

WHO OWNS THIS? Default owner varies according to local copyright law – could be label or artist – though artist will often transfer ownership and/or control to another party.

WHAT RIGHTS? The copyright provides a number of 'controls', all of which will usually be transferred to a record label. However, the artist's separate right to 'equitable remuneration' (ER) on performing rights revenue cannot usually be transferred to the label.

ALL ELEMENTS OF THE RECORDING COPYRIGHT	ARTIST'S 'ER' RIGHT ON PERFORMING RIGHTS INCOME
RECORD LABEL	ARTISTS' CMO (PPL in the UK)
Label either licenses direct or via a CMO (PPL in UK)	CMO collects Performer ER
Label pays royalty to featured artist according to record contract	CMO passes Performer ER income to both featured artist and sessions musicians

*Default ownership and equitable remuneration rules, and the way the different elements of the song right are split, varies from country to country. And, of course, artists and songwriters don't only create when sent into the studio by a label!

also enjoy other rights directly from copyright law, commonly called moral and performer rights. For recording artists, the most common performer rights relate to 'approvals' and 'performer equitable remuneration'.

Approval must usually be gained to record an artist's performance and to then exploit that recording. Artists may also often enjoy an automatic (ie non-contractual and non-waivable) right to share in certain (though not all) revenue streams associated with their recordings, most often performing rights income.

Licensees should be aware of these additional creator and performer rights, which co-exist with the actual copyright that will likely be controlled by a corporate entity.

6. Digital Licensing

In the physical product domain, a record company exploited its own sound recording copyright, and licensed the rights to exploit the accompanying song copyright from the relevant music publisher or publishers, usually via the collective licensing system. The CD was then provided to the retailer 'rights ready'.

With just a few exceptions, in the digital domain, download stores and streaming services need to have separate licensing relationships with both record companies and music publishers and/or their respective CMOs. Labels generally license all but online radio directly, though personalised radio services may also be licensed by the CMO in some territories (especially the US,

where a compulsory licence applies). Publishers license most digital services collectively, though the big publishers now often license Anglo-American repertoire directly, albeit via joint venture vehicles with the CMOs.

As an extra complication, downloads and streams exploit both the reproduction rights and the performing rights of the copyright.

On the publishing side, this is important because these two elements of the copyright are often licensed separately (remember, in the UK PRS controls the performing right and the publisher the reproduction right).

In many countries, publishers usually try to provide digital services with 'combined rights licenses', which means that, where reproduction and performing rights are controlled by different entities, those two entities need to work together. For example, where publishers license digital direct, they must do so in partnership with the CMOs which control the performing rights.

On the recordings side, the label is able to license both elements of the copyright, though because performer equitable remuneration is often due on performing rights income but not reproduction rights income, the fact that both elements of the copyright are being exploited is still relevant. Except, most labels argue that a specific and separate performing right, first introduced in the mid 1990s and called the 'making available right', is what the digital platforms

> **66 the deal between the rights owner and the streaming platform is ultimately a revenue share arrangement ... every deal is different, and usually secret, though labels generally see 50-60% of revenue allocated to their catalogue whereas publishers see 10-15%99**

actually exploit, and that that is exempt from performer equitable remuneration. Not all artists agree.

7. The Streaming Deal

Most streaming services are licensed in more or less the same way. The deal between the rights owner and the streaming platform is ultimately a revenue share arrangement.

Each month the streaming service works out what percentage of overall consumption came from any one label or publisher's catalogue. It then allocates that percentage of its overall advertising and/or subscription revenue (after sales tax) to the rights owner, and pays them a cut based on a pre-existing revenue share arrangement. Every deal is different, and usually secret, though labels generally see 50-60% of revenue allocated to their catalogue whereas publishers see 10-15%. Overall the streaming service aims to retain about 30%.

In addition to the core revenue share arrangement, rights owners

will usually seek to minimise their risk by having the streaming service pay minimum rates, for example an amount per play, so that they are guaranteed certain income based on consumption oblivious of the streaming service's revenues. Rights owners will also often demand upfront advances from the streaming services, while labels may seek equity in start up services and other kickbacks.

8. Money Flow

Payment of streaming royalties can be complex. Streaming services generally assume that whichever label provided it with a track owns the copyright, and pays that label its share of the revenue, or the minimum guarantee, whichever is higher.

The label will then usually be obliged to share that income with the artist, subject to the terms of said artist's record deal. Most labels pay artists the same share on digital income as physical income, or maybe a few per cent more. There has been much debate as to whether this is fair, while some artists with pre-digital record

> **66 every record deal is different, but usually artists will receive a minority cut of income – commonly 15-20% – and only after some or all of the label's initial and ongoing costs have been paid ... there is some confusion in the artist and management community as to what ongoing costs many labels are deducting from digital income 99**

contracts argue this is an incorrect interpretation of their original agreements.

Every record deal is different, but usually artists will receive a minority cut of income – commonly 15-20% in modern UK deals (often much lower in older deals) – and only after some or all of the label's initial and ongoing costs have been paid (exact terms are set out in the record contract). There is some confusion in the artist and management community as to what ongoing costs many labels are deducting from digital income.

On the publishing side, the streaming service does not usually know which publisher or publishers own the rights in any one song. Therefore the streaming service reports all consumption to each licensor. The rights owner then calculates what it is due and invoices the streaming

service, which then needs to ensure it isn't being invoiced twice for the same song (or that two licensors aren't both claiming to own 60% of a song).

Once the publishing sector has been paid, money then needs to be split between the performing and reproduction rights.

What happens next depends on the country. In the UK, performing rights income goes to PRS, which pays 50% to songwriter and 50% to publisher. Reproduction rights income goes to the publisher (sometimes via MCPS) which will pay a share to the songwriter according to their publishing contract.

ISSUES

The interviews and artist manager survey conducted during Part One of the 'Dissecting The Digital Dollar' project identified a number of issues with the current streaming model that the music industry needs to address. These were the issues discussed at the subsequent roundtable debates.

1. Division of streaming revenue

Is the division of streaming income between each of the stakeholders fair? This includes the split between the streaming services and the music community, between the recording and the song rights, between the reproduction and the performing rights, and between the artist and the label.

2. Performer equitable remuneration and making available

Performer rights in many countries say that all artists are due equitable remuneration when their 'performing rights' are exploited.

However, as mentioned above, most labels argue that digital services exploit a specific and separate performing right called the 'making available right', and that equitable remuneration is not due on this income.

Not all artists agree, while some acts with pre-1990s record contacts argue that labels cannot exploit this right anyway without their specific approval (though most do).

3. Sharing the value of digital deals

Labels, publishers and CMOs have created templates for streaming service deals, with revenue share arrangements, minimum guarantees, advances, equity and other kickbacks. Managers feel that artists are sometimes being unfairly excluded from profits generated by upfront elements of the deal like advances and equity.

4. Transparency

Artists, songwriters and their managers are also often kept in the dark about the specifics of the agreements reached between the labels, publishers and CMOs and the DSPs and they are rarely consulted on the merits of each component of the deal. This despite artists and songwriters being beneficiaries of these deals.

5. Safe harbours and opt-out services

While some streaming services only carry content provided by label partners, others – including YouTube and SoundCloud – allow users to upload content. Rights owners can then request that content be removed, or allow it to remain for promotional purposes, or – if the user-upload platform allows – choose to monetise the uploaded content.

These services rely on the so called 'safe harbours' in US and European law to avoid financial and criminal liability for copyright infringement while hosting unlicensed material users have uploaded. Some question whether the safe harbours were designed for this purpose, and whether the existence of 'opt-out' streaming services of this kind is distorting the wider digital music market.

6. Data

The music industry is now having to process unprecedented amounts of data, as revenues and royalties are increasingly based on consumption rather than sales. The lack of decent copyright ownership data also hinders efficiency, especially on the publishing side. There are almost certainly 'big data' solutions to these problems – and numerous entities are now working on such solutions – though the question remains as to who should lead on this activity. And will labels, publishers and CMOs share the crucial copyright ownership data that is in their control?

7. Collective licensing

The labels license most digital services directly, while the publishers often use their CMOs. For various reasons, both artists and songwriters often prefer money to go through the CMOs rather than their labels and publishers, though there is an argument that this is not always the most efficient way to process revenue and data. Either way, artists and songwriters often feel excluded from the debate over the pros and cons of collective licensing.

8. Adapting to the new business models

One of the biggest challenges for everyone in the music community is simply adapting to a new way of doing business, where sustained listening rather than first week sales

matter, and where successful tracks and albums will deliver revenues over a longer period of time, rather than via a short-term spike. Adapting to this new way of doing business is arguably just a fact of life, though some stakeholders may be shielded more than others from any short-term negative impact.

QUESTIONS

As we said, the aim of 'Dissecting The Digital Dollar' was to inform and initiate debate. From the issues we identified, we then posed fifteen key questions for the wider music industry to consider and answer. Many of these were then discussed at the roundtable debates, the key findings of which are included in section seven on this book.

The fifteen questions were as follows:

1. How should digital income be split between the music industry and the digital platforms themselves?

2. Of the 65-75% of streaming revenues paid to the music industry, how should these monies be split between the two copyrights, ie the recordings and the songs?

3. Downloads and streams exploit both the reproduction and communication controls of the copyright – ie both the reproduction and the performing rights. How should income be allocated between the two elements of each copyright?

4. Where a record label owns the copyright in a sound recording but pays a royalty to the featured artist

THE DIGITAL DOLLAR ISSUES

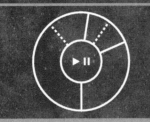

DIVISION OF REVENUE

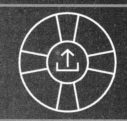

SAFE HARBOUR

PERFORMER ER

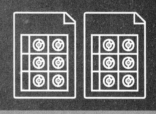

COPYRIGHT DATA

SHARING THE VALUE

COLLECTIVE LICENSING

TRANSPARENCY

THE NEW MODEL

under the terms of their record contract, what royalty should the label pay on downloads and streams compared to CDs?

5. What kind of digital services exploit the conventional performing rights and what kind exploit the specific 'making available right', and should copyright law be more specific on this point?

6. Should performer equitable remuneration apply to all streaming services, including those exploiting the making available right?

7. Do record labels need a specific making available waiver from all artists before exploiting their recordings digitally?

8. Should record companies and music publishers demand equity from digital start-ups, and if so should they share the profits of any subsequent share sale with their artists and songwriters, and if so on what terms?

9. Should record companies and music publishers demand large advances from new digital services, and if so should they share any 'breakage' (unallocated advances) with their artists and songwriters, and if so on what terms?

10. Should record companies and music publishers demand other kickbacks from new digital services, and if so should they share the benefits with their artists, and if so on what terms?

11. Can it be right that the beneficiaries of copyright are not allowed to know how their songs and recordings are being monetised, and should a new performer or moral right ensure that information is made available to artists, songwriters and their representatives?

12. Should the safe harbours in European and American law be revised so companies like YouTube and SoundCloud cannot benefit from them, however good their takedown systems may or may not be?

13. How is the music rights industry rising to the challenge of processing usage data and royalty payments from streaming services, what data demands should artists and songwriters be making of their labels, publishers and CMOs, and is a central database of copyright ownership ultimately required?

14. Are streaming services best licensed direct or through collective management organisations; if direct what is the best solution when societies actually control elements of the copyright; and are artists and songwriters actually told what solutions have been adopted?

15. Is the biggest challenge for the music industry simply adapting to a new business model which pays out based on consumption rather than sales, and over a much longer time period; and what can artists and songwriters do to better adapt?

SECTION TWO:
MUSIC RIGHTS & CONTROLS

Copyright is ultimately about providing creators with certain controls over that which they create, either as a point of principle, and/or to encourage and enable creativity by allowing creators and their business partners to exploit these controls for profit.

2.1 THE KEY MUSIC RIGHTS

The music industry owns and exploits two distinct sets of copyright[1]:

▶ The copyright in songs (lyrics and musical compositions) – known as 'author rights' under civil law systems and generally referred to as 'publishing rights' within the music industry.

▶ The copyright in sound recordings – known as 'neighbouring rights' under many civil law systems and generally referred to as the 'recording' or 'master rights' by the music business.

The distinction is important for various reasons:

▶ In some countries, copyright law will apply different rules to the publishing rights and the recording rights. For example, in the US, AM and FM radio stations must secure licences from and pay royalties to publishing rights owners, but they do not need to pay similar royalties to recording rights owners[2].

▶ Even when that is not the case, the music industry itself will treat the publishing rights and recording rights differently, and will often license them in different ways. This is especially true when it comes to so called 'collective licensing'.

▶ Whilst many music rights businesses deal in both publishing and recording rights, they will usually do so through separate autonomous companies. Anyone wishing to make use of recordings of songs will need to deal with both entities.

▶ Whilst many artists will be involved in the creation of both songs and recordings[3], they will often work with different companies to exploit the two sets of rights – so will negotiate separate publishing and record deals with two completely separate

1: The music industry controls plenty of other kinds of intellectual property too – including audio-visual, artistic and other literary works – but these are the core music rights that this report will focus on.

2: The US record industry is currently lobbying to change this so to move into line with the rest of the world.

3: In our survey of artist managers, 93% of the acts they represent are involved in the creation of both songs and recordings.

The core music rights

RECORDING RIGHTS
AKA MASTER RIGHTS

- RECORDING ARTISTS
- RECORD PRODUCERS
- RECORD LABELS
- MUSIC DISTRIBUTORS
- CMOs (for labels)
- CMOs (for performers)

THE RECORD INDUSTRY

PUBLISHING RIGHTS
AKA SONG RIGHTS

- SONGWRITERS
- COMPOSERS
- MUSIC PUBLISHERS
- ADMINISTRATORS
- CMOs (performing rights)
- CMOs (mechanical rights)

THE MUSIC PUBLISHING SECTOR

businesses. By convention, key elements of these two deals will usually differ, in that publishing deals tend to be more generous to songwriters than record deals are to artists, for reasons we will explain below.

▶ The music rights industry can therefore be split into two: the 'music publishing industry' controlling and exploiting song copyrights, and the 'record industry' controlling and exploiting recording copyrights.

2.2 COPYRIGHT CONTROLS

Copyright law provides rights owners with a number of 'controls' over how each piece of content they own is used.

Copyright law does not usually refer to these controls as 'controls' – UK copyright law calls them "acts restricted by the copyright" [4] – but terminology varies from country to country and here we will use the word 'control' as a clear and neutral term.

The exact list of controls also varies around the world, and sometimes differs between publishing and recording rights. The UK system lists six distinct controls, most of which can be identified, in one form or another, in other copyright systems too.

They are as follows...

▶ **The Reproduction Control** is the true 'copy' right, in that it gives the rights owner the exclusive right to make copies of a work.

▶ **The Distribution Control** provides the rights owner with the exclusive right to issue copies of a work to the public [5].

▶ **The Rental Control** provides the rights owner with the exclusive right to rent or lend copies of a work to the public.

▶ **The Adaptation Control** provides the rights owner with the exclusive right to make adaptations of a work.

▶ **The Performance Control** provides the rights owner with the exclusive right to perform or display a work in public (with 'public' usually being defined widely to cover pretty much anything outside the private home or car).

▶ **The Communication Control** provides the rights owner with the exclusive right to communicate a work to the public, which traditionally means broadcast but also covers communication through digital channels (the latter sometimes being referred to specifically as the separate 'making available' control, depending on how the user accesses the content).

In the music industry, the reproduction and distribution controls (or similar) are often grouped

---

4: Copyright, Designs And Patents Act 1988 Section 16.

5: Though this right is usually limited so that the rights owner has no control over the subsequent resale of copies it first issued (providing no additional copying is required to resell, so this principally applies to physical copies).

Copyright controls

REPRODUCTION OR MECHANICAL RIGHTS

REPRODUCTION CONTROL

DISTRIBUTION CONTROL

RENTAL CONTROL

ADAPTATION CONTROL

PERFORMANCE CONTROL

COMMUNICATION CONTROL

MAKING AVAILABLE CONTROL

PERFORMING OR NEIGHBOURING RIGHTS

together and called the 'reproduction rights' or 'mechanical rights'. We will use the former as a neutral term in this book, because within the music business the term 'mechanical rights' tends to be associated more with songs than recordings.

The music industry also usually groups together the performance and communication controls (or similar) and calls them the 'performing rights' or 'neighbouring rights'.

Again, we will use the former as a neutral term in this book, because while 'neighbouring rights' is an increasingly popular phrase in the record industry, the term is confusing because of its different definition under some civil law systems (as mentioned above).

Which copyright control or controls are being exploited at any one time is important because, again, the rules set out in copyright law may differ depending on which specific control is in play, and even when that isn't the case the music industry itself routinely treats and manages each control, or set of controls, differently.

2.3 HOW COPYRIGHTS MAKE MONEY

Copyrights make money when third parties – called licensees – want to exploit one or more of these controls: so they want to copy a work, or adapt it, or perform it, or communicate it, and so on.

Because the copyright owner has the exclusive right to exploit their content in any of these ways, the third party needs to seek permission[6]. And permission is usually granted in return for payment.

Licensees may want to exploit more than one copyright – and more than one control – at any one time. For example:

▶ If a third party wants to make a copy of a recording of a song, they are exploiting the separate copyrights in the recording and the song, and therefore need to secure permission for both.

▶ If a third party wants to stream a track, they are exploiting both the reproduction and communication controls of both the recording and song copyrights, and need

---

6: Copyright law routinely provides certain scenarios where permission is not, in fact, required, such as private copies, critical analysis or parody. These are usually called copyright 'exceptions' or 'exemptions', or 'fair use' and 'fair dealing', and again rules vary from country to country.

7: This in itself can be challenging, as generally copyright ownership is not registered with any statutory body (international copyright treaties say registration is not required) and there is no one-stop-shop copyright ownership database provided by the music industry.

8: Though not always; a rights owner may simply wish not to do a deal, or more likely the artist or songwriter involved in creating a recording or song may have a contractual veto right that stops a corporate rights owner entering into a certain kind of deal without their permission, and the artist or songwriter may exercise that veto for ethical, reputational or other reasons.

9: In that the record companies and music publishers appoint separate CMOs, even though many licensees need to exploit both sets of rights. In some countries record industry and publishing sector societies may offer at least some joint licensees – the number of these joint licences is increasing.

to ensure all the right permissions are secured.

2.4 DIRECT, COLLECTIVE AND COMPULSORY LICENCES

When a third party wants to exploit a copyright work they must get a licence – so permission – from the copyright owner or owners.

At a basic level, the licensee must identify and locate the rights owners[7] and then negotiate terms.

The rights owner will usually demand some form of payment in return for granting a licence. Levels of payment can vary greatly.

The rights owner can usually ask for whatever sum of money they like, though – assuming they are seeking to do a deal, which most rights owners are[8] – they are constrained by market realities, such as what the licensee can realistically afford and how important it is to the licensee that this specific deal is done.

But beyond these commercial constraints, in most countries copyright law does not generally seek to particularly regulate these directly negotiated deals.

COLLECTIVE LICENSING

However, in some circumstances the music industry chooses to license collectively. This is where a large number of rights owners decide – instead of doing direct deals with each and every individual licensee – to put all their rights into one pot and appoint a standalone organisation to license on their behalf.

These organisations are often referred to as 'collecting societies', or 'performing rights organisations' (PROs), or 'collective management organisations' (CMOs). We will generally use the latter term.

The CMO then agrees terms with licensees (often with whole groups of licensees together), collects any monies that are due, and distributes income back to the rights owners often (though not always) based on what songs or recordings are used.

The music industry generally chooses to license collectively for practical reasons. Mainly to reduce legal and administration costs where you have a set of licensees that is either large or which uses a lot of music, or both, but where per-usage or per-licence income is relatively modest. Or where direct licensing would simply be impractical, or unenforceable, and would likely lead to music being used without license resulting in lost income overall.

Both the record industry and the music publishing sector routinely license collectively, though separately[9]: radio stations, clubs, jukebox operators and public spaces that play recorded music. TV sync is also often licensed through the collective licensing system by both the record labels and publishers.

The publishers also usually license collectively the live performance of songs in public and the reproduction and distribution of recordings of published songs. Though precise rules can vary from CMO to CMO, and territory to territory.

THE REGULATION OF COLLECTIVE LICENSING

Legislators generally support collective licensing, despite the market power it arguably gives the CMOs, because of the convenience it provides the potential licensee. Nevertheless, such an approach does create competition law concerns, because if all rights owners license as one, the licensee has nowhere else to go to secure a licence, which could potentially lead to anti-competitive behaviour.

For this reason collective licensing is often subject to further regulation, which might include provisions for licensing negotiations to be escalated to a 'copyright tribunal', or similar authority, which has the power to rule on royalty disputes and therefore ultimately set the rates a licensee must pay. Collective licensing rules again vary from country to country.

COMPULSORY LICENSES

In some countries copyright law instigates a number of compulsory licences, specific scenarios in which rights owners are obliged to issue a licence. For example, rights owners are often obliged to license radio stations via a compulsory licence, while record labels in the US are obliged by copyright law to license personalised radio services such as Pandora.

Where such licences apply, rights owners are still due payment for the use of their content, but they lose the right to walk away from deal negotiations, which obviously weakens their negotiating hand somewhat. Rights owners usually provide compulsory licences through the collective licensing system, and are often obliged to do so under law, with copyright courts or statutory bodies ultimately setting rates.

SECTION THREE:
OWNERSHIP & ROYALTIES

Unlike other forms of intellectual property, copyrights are not usually registered with a statutory authority[10], rather copyright 'crystallises' when a work is 'fixed' in material form[11], providing certain criteria are met.

Because of this, copyright law provides rules or guidance on who the 'default' or 'presumed' owners may be, ie when a work is fixed and the copyright crystallises, who by default owns the copyright? These rules vary from country to country, and according to the kind of copyright.

3.1 DEFAULT OWNERSHIP RULES

Generally with lyrics and musical compositions the default owners are the lyricist and the composer, ie the 'creator' or 'author'. Co-written works are co-owned by all parties, though it's for the creators to decide on how the copyright is split between each contributor[12]. The main exception here is when a work is created by an employee as part of their job description – often called 'work for hire' in the US – in which case the employer may be the default copyright owner, depending on local rules[13].

With sound recordings, default ownership rules vary from copyright system to copyright system. In some countries, the individual or company that funds (ie pays for) a recording, rather than the performers who appear on it, will be the default owner

of the resulting copyright. These funders, usually record labels, are often referred to in copyright law as the 'producer', but shouldn't be confused with studio producers.

It's also worth noting that, where performers are, by default, owners or co-owners of recording rights, statutory provisions or work for hire clauses within contracts may take effect, making the label essentially their employer and, as their employer, the default owner.

3.2 ASSIGNMENT

Although the law provides default ownership rules, the default owner can usually transfer ownership of their copyrights (both existing and future) to other parties, usually in return for money.

Many systems allow full transfer of ownership, usually called 'assignment'. Even where this is not possible, such as in Germany, copyrights can be licensed in their entirety to a third party, which practically amounts to the same thing[14].

When record companies and music publishers sign new talent who will inevitably require some sort of upfront investment (eg an advance, artist development, marketing) with no real guarantee of a return, the corporate entities will usually seek outright ownership of all the copyrights created under that first contract or, in the case of publishing, outright ownership of at least some elements of the copyright (that is to say, ownership of some of the controls outlined above, and a revenue share from any others, more on which below).

Any resulting agreement will be structured in such a way as to make the label or publisher actual or de facto rights owner according to copyright law in the local jurisdiction. Of course the record company may be the default owner of the sound recording copyrights by statute anyway, but agreements will be written to avoid any ambiguity.

Copyrights don't last forever, but usually have pretty long terms (50-95 years from release for recordings, and life of the creator plus 50-70 years – sometimes longer – for songs[15]). With new talent record deals, the label may want ownership for 'life of copyright'. In publishing contracts though, even with new talent deals, rights are more likely to revert to the songwriter at some point – by law in the US, or by agreement elsewhere – albeit possibly after a significant period of time.

An artist or songwriter who assigns their rights may also, if successful, be able to renegotiate contracts at a later date giving them ownership or co-ownership of any copyrights created, though this is not usually a given in first deal contracts.

3.3 THE CONTRACTUAL RIGHTS OF ARTISTS AND SONGWRITERS

Although artists and songwriters routinely assign[16] – and therefore give up – the copyright in works they created to record companies and music publishers, they will likely retain certain contractual rights over or in relation to those works. These

---

10: Statutory or commercial copyright registries do exist in some countries, but logging works with them is usually voluntary. In the US, certain remedies are not available in court for unregistered works (though this mainly applies to domestic rather than foreign works).

11: So, it is transcribed, recorded, filmed, etc.

12: Though if two people collaborate with one writing the lyrics and the other writing the musical composition, under some copyright systems – such as the UK – they each own outright their respective copyright, ie the copyright in the lyrics and the separate copyright in the composition. But if they both contribute to both the lyrics and the score in a manner whereby their individual contributions cannot be separately identified, they would both co-own both copyrights.

13: Where this is the case, copyright law and/or case law will normally provide a definition of what constitutes an 'employee' in this context, and/or when 'work for hire' applies.

14: There may be some significant differences though, such as what happens if a licensee goes into liquidation, though day-to-day the corporate licensee acts as if it owns the copyright.

15: Where there are multiple creators, the copyright term is usually 70 years after the last surviving collaborator dies.

16: Or similar, such as exclusive licence in perpetuity.

will be set out in their assignment contract (or similar).

It is worth mentioning that, on the sound recordings side, it is so called 'featured artists'[17] who routinely retain rights of this nature through contract. Session musicians who appear on recordings will often be paid a set fee for their time and then have no future involvement in the exploitation of their work.

Both featured artists and session musicians still enjoy 'performer rights' under law (more on which in section four), but it is generally the former that also benefit from the contractual rights we are about to discuss (studio producers do often get a royalty from recordings they produce, but other rights may be limited).

ROYALTIES

The most important of these contractual rights relate to royalties, ie the artist or songwriter's right to share in any money generated by the exploitation of any copyrights they helped create.

A record and publishing contract will usually state that featured artists and songwriters must receive a share of any revenue generated by their work. How payments are calculated and paid, and what percentage the artist or songwriter receives, will vary from contract to contract, and within the contract will often vary according to how revenue is generated.

The label and publisher will also usually have the right to recoup (often exclusively from the artist's share of revenue) some or all of their upfront costs, which includes any advances paid, before any income is shared at all, and will often have the right to deduct other ongoing costs from revenues before any royalties due to the artist or songwriter are paid.

There are some extra points to note here too.

▶ Firstly, newer record deals may also give the label a cut of revenue generated by the artist beyond their sound recordings, such as live activity or merchandise for example. These are often called '360 degree deals' and the other income streams the label shares in are referred to as 'ancillary revenues' or 'non-recorded income'. Each contract needs to state whether ancillary revenues do or do not count towards the label's unrecouped costs.

▶ Secondly, in publishing, some elements of the copyright will likely be allocated – or actually assigned – to a CMO, which will then usually pay the songwriter their share of subsequent revenue directly. This often means that the songwriter receives their share of this income from day one, ie payment is not subject to recoupment. The publisher has to recoup its investment from those revenue streams not allocated to the CMO.

17: Featured artists are the musicians whose name or names any one recording is released under, as opposed to session musicians who are simply credited in the small print. Record labels generally sign record deals with featured artists.

▶ Outside the US, there is usually a direct contract between the songwriter and the CMO covering those elements of the copyright assigned to the society. The songwriter's publishing contract then does two things: it assigns those elements of the copyright not allocated to the CMO to the publisher, and gives the publisher a simple contractual right to share in the revenue generated by the elements that the CMO controls.

▶ What rights the CMO actually controls, how songwriters are paid, and whether or not these payments are subject to recoupment, varies according to the operating mandate and internal rules of each society.

Every contract is different, and more established artists and songwriters will usually secure better deals than new talent.

Though as a general rule, record contracts are tipped in the label's favour, allowing them to keep the majority of revenues generated, whereas publishing contracts are likely to be more favourable to the songwriter.

Record labels would justify this by arguing that they usually take a much bigger financial risk than the publisher, especially when working with new artists.

It is worth noting that the calculation and payment of royalties by labels and publishers is a common cause of tension between music rights companies and the artists and songwriters they work with, especially when artists have stopped working with a label on creating new content, but are still receiving royalties from past assignment deals.

Many artists believe that their business partners are "twisting the rules" or "playing the system" – actively or through inactivity – to reduce the royalties they have to pay out. After all, once a label no longer requires an artist to create or promote new content, arguably it has little incentive to interpret or fulfill contractual obligations in a way that favours artists over its shareholders.

Record and publishing contracts usually provide artists and songwriters with the right to audit a label or publisher, but in real terms many artists cannot afford to enforce this right effectively. And where there are contractual ambiguities, many artists will be nervous about pursuing expensive litigation, given the big rights owners are nearly always better resourced to fight such legal battles (and if an artist is well resourced, labels and publishers may agree to secret deals to avoid test cases in court and the resulting precedent).

VETOES AND OTHER CONTRACTUAL RIGHTS

In addition to royalties, record and publishing contracts may give talent other rights too. This includes rights to consultation and approval (what might amount to a veto), which provide artists and songwriters with certain controls over how their content is exploited.

A veto right usually requires a label or publisher to get specific approval from an artist or songwriter before allowing their work to be used in specific scenarios, eg in an advert or on a new digital platform. Vetoes vary from contract to contract – some are in the artist's absolute discretion, some are subject to the artist being 'reasonable' – and more established artists will negotiate more of these rights into their deals.

3.4 DISTRIBUTION AND ADMINISTRATION DEALS

Of course songwriters and artists can choose to retain ownership of all the copyrights in the songs and recordings they create, and many do. Though new talent may struggle to find a label or publisher willing to pay a cash advance, and to invest in artist development, content production and marketing activities, without receiving a copyright assignment in return (or the equivalent under local copyright law).

But where artists and songwriters require less or no upfront investment, they can engage the services of a label and publisher while retaining copyright ownership through what were traditionally known in the record industry as 'distribution deals' and in the music publishing sector as 'administration deals', but which may now be called a 'licensing' or 'services' deal.

Many labels and publishers will provide creative, administrative, distribution and marketing services on a fee or revenue share basis without assignment where their risk is minimised; indeed many labels have separate divisions to work with artists on this basis.

In addition to that, a big growth area in the music rights sector has been in the 'label services' domain, that is to say standalone companies that provide rights management, distribution and/or marketing services, sometimes to other labels and publishers, but increasingly directly to artists and songwriters.

A by-product of this is that while artists and songwriters – and especially more established talent – may retain ownership of their copyrights, they will usually appoint a label, publisher and/or other service provider to manage and represent their rights. Said companies will then be mandated to act as if they owned those copyrights until any deal with the artist or songwriter expires.

3.5 THE ROLE OF CMOS

The aforementioned CMOs also act as rights owners, sometimes actually and other times as agents. As explained above, the CMOs are usually involved where the music industry decides to license collectively rather than via direct deals.

RECORDINGS V PUBLISHING RIGHTS

In any one country, the record and music publishing industries will each appoint one or more CMOs to represent their interests in collective licensing scenarios. In most cases, record companies and music publishers have formed separate CMOs, meaning that licensees making use of recordings of songs will usually need to seek separate licences from at least two societies.

PERFORMING V REPRODUCTION RIGHTS

Meanwhile, in the publishing sector, a distinction is often made between the collective licensing of reproduction rights and the collective licensing of performing rights, with autonomous divisions of the same societies – or totally separate CMOs – appointed for each set of rights.

NOT ALL CMOS ARE THE SAME

Although all CMOs are basically providing the same services for their members – negotiating deals, analysing data and distributing revenue – the status, structure, membership and power of the societies varies from country to country, and between the record industry and the music publishing sector.

A key differentiator is the aforementioned convention in the song rights domain whereby songwriters, outside the US, actually allocate some elements of their copyrights to a society rather than a publisher. Where this occurs, the songwriter is giving the CMO the exclusive global right to represent those elements of his or her copyrights, and the publisher is simply a beneficiary of those rights.

This means two things. First, these CMOs are not simply agents for corporate rights owners that negotiate deals wherever collective licensing is employed, they actually control the rights they represent. Second, both songwriters and publishers are members of the society, and the CMO will be governed by a board made up of both songwriter and publisher members. Both these facts arguably make these CMOs more powerful.

Aside from the UK and Italy, songwriters and composers actually constitute a majority on the board of all the CMOs in the European Union. Nevertheless, many songwriters believe the publishers have more influence at board level, which, if true, may simply be due to publisher board members having greater business expertise. But either way, the society must be representative, and be seen to be representative, of both songwriter and publisher members.

Not all CMOs representing song rights are structured in this way. The US societies operate differently, and in those countries where reproduction rights are managed by separate CMOs, these may also differ. For example, in the UK, PRS represents performing rights and is structured as just described, but MCPS represents reproduction rights and its board consists mainly of publishers, and it acts more as an agent for its members than an actual copyright owner.

In the record industry, where record companies control both the performing and reproduction rights, the labels' CMOs again usually act as simple agents for the corporate rights owners wherever collective licensing applies. Artists are not normally members of these societies, though the artist community in each country will usually have their own CMO to collect revenue associated with their performer rights, more on which in section four below (in the UK and US, the same societies that represent the labels, PPL and SoundExchange respectively, also administer some or all performer rights income).

Perhaps the most important difference between those CMOs which are assigned rights versus those which act as agents for corporate rights owners, is that labels and publishers could in theory unilaterally withdraw their repertoires from the latter (where compulsory licences do not apply of course, and subject to the society's own rules), whereas publishers could never unilaterally withdraw from CMOs which have been assigned rights by songwriters.

COLLECTIVE LICENSING WORLDWIDE

Where collective licensing applies, rights owners traditionally appoint their local CMOs to issue licenses to individuals and companies operating in their home territory.

CMOs commonly provide licensees with a 'blanket licence', which allows them to make use of all and any of the songs or recordings in the society's repertoire, on either a fixed-fee-per-usage or revenue share basis. Participation in these blanket

licences is often then compulsory for all society members.

Of course more prolific licensees will likely require access to more than just domestic repertoire, so reciprocal agreements are made between CMOs around the world, meaning that in any one market the local society is empowered to license songs or recordings from all over the globe. Revenues are then passed onto foreign societies if and when songs or recordings in their repertoire are exploited by a licensee.

This arrangement gives users operating under a blanket licence permission to use a vast catalogue of songs and recordings. So vast, in fact, that even though there will be gaps in the repertoire (where a rights owner hasn't affiliated with a society or where reciprocal agreements between two countries are yet to be made), many licensees assume the licence allows them to legally use any song or recording that is protected by copyright.

Traditionally reciprocal agreements usually only allowed a CMO to license the repertoire of other societies in its home territory. So while a society can license something nearing a global catalogue in its home country, it can only license its own repertoire worldwide (and only then if expressly empowered to do so by its members). This usually means that a licensee operating in multiple territories must seek separate licences in each country via the local society (and for all rights and controls as required).

This has proven challenging in the digital era, where many more licensees seek to operate in multiple countries.

Some of the publishing sector's CMOs have sought to provide multi-territory licenses, partly in response to licensee demand and, in Europe, partly to accommodate the European Commission, which says that societies within the European Union should compete for members and licensees in order to comply with competition law.

There is an ever incresing number of these multi-territory licences now available, especially in Europe, meanwhile reciprocal agreements and CMO licensing conventions also continue to evolve.

3.6 COMPLEXITY THROUGH FLEXIBILITY

Copyright law does not usually seek to regulate the specifics of assignment or licensing agreements, or how the ownership and control of individual copyrights is divided and transferred. This flexibility is a good thing, but it results in complexity.

An artist, songwriter or rights owner may assign or license their copyrights to different entities in different countries; they may assign or license their rights for a set period of time rather that the full copyright term; and they may assign each element of the copyright – so each control – separately to different parties.

Rights owners can appoint CMOs or other middle men for some licensing scenarios, but continue to deal direct in others[18]. And entities which acquire copyrights are usually at liberty to sell them on to other parties down the line.

And, of course, you have co-ownership of copyright. This is particularly important with song copyrights, because collaboration is common in songwriting, and collaborating creators – and their publishers and CMOs – will share in the copyrights they create. The law doesn't dictate what the split in ownership might be, instead this is agreed between participating parties. But there is no one central repository where these agreements are documented and there may be disagreements regarding agreed splits after the fact.

THE DATA DILEMMA

Finding accurate and comprehensive data detailing who owns and controls copyright works is a significant issue, because there are so many variables and, in most countries, no formal registration of rights.

Numerous companies and organisations, and especially the CMOs, have their own databases listing who owns what song or recording copyrights. But few of these databases are publicly available, and no one database lists every song and recording. And information (especially in relation to

18: Collective licensing regulations and individual CMO rules may limit rights owners' abilities to opt in and out of collective dealing, though there is generally some flexibility across the wider copyright.

splits in co-owned works) may differ from one database to another, with no central authority to deal with such conflicts.

Efforts by the music publishing sector to form a single Global Repertoire Database (GRD) collapsed in 2014. Even if it had succeeded, that database would have only covered song copyrights, and would have then had to be linked to the record industry's databases.

The need for a good central publicly accessible music rights database has only increased since then, especially as streaming has come to dominate the recorded music business.

Various entities, including CMOs, are involved in projects to try and address this issue, in some cases by developing 'regional repertoire databases' (RRDs) that may one day merge to create the ambitious Global Repertoire Database.

It is too early to tell which of these will succeed, or whether any data project will truly solve the data problem.

SECTION FOUR:
PERFORMER RIGHTS & EQUITABLE REMUNERATION

As well as providing rights owners with a series of controls over how their content is utilised and distributed, copyright law also often gives creators and performers certain additional and concurrent controls over any of the works they help create, even (and especially) when they have no claim to the actual copyright in those works.

These controls are often called 'moral rights' or 'performer rights'. The extent and positioning of these rights varies greatly from country to country, though a key consideration is whether or not they can be waived in a record or publishing contract. Where they can be waived, corporate rights owners will usually insist that they are, which may make these rights ineffective in real terms.

The evolution of the so called performer rights in the digital era is a particularly interesting area.

In most countries two main sets of performer rights exist, which originate in the Rome Convention of 1961 (though in many cases formalised more recently than that) and apply to all artists who participate in a sound recording, including both featured artists and session musicians (and, in some cases, the studio producer, depending on their involvement).

Terminology will vary from country to country, but we will refer to these two sets of rights as Performer Approvals and Performer Equitable Remuneration (or Performer ER).

PERFORMER APPROVALS

Performers enjoy certain controls in relation to their sound recordings, from the initial 'fixation' of the recording itself to any subsequent exploitation by the copyright owner or third parties.

These controls are usually similar or identical to the controls enjoyed by the actual copyright owner as defined in section two above, though will also include that initial 'fixation control', ie the right to make a recording of a performance at all.

In real terms these controls take the form of 'approvals', in that a copyright owner must secure the approval of all performers (or, in some cases, secure the assignment of this performer right from the artist) to make and subsequently exploit a recording. These approvals (or assignments) are usually gained from featured artists through their record contracts, and from session musicians on a case-by-case basis.

Where approval is not sought, a record company, say, has no right to

Performer controls

- FIXATION CONTROL
- REPRODUCTION CONTROL
- DISTRIBUTION CONTROL
- RENTAL CONTROL
- ADAPTATION CONTROL
- PERFORMANCE CONTROL
- COMMUNICATION CONTROL
- MAKING AVAILABLE CONTROL

make a recording of a performance, or to subsequently exploit it, even if they are clearly the copyright owner according to default ownership rules.

PERFORMER ER

Performers also usually have a right to 'equitable remuneration' from certain specific exploitations of their recordings, most commonly the exploitation of performing rights (ie the public performance and communication controls). Of course artists may be due a share of income generated by their recordings through contract anyway, but this performer right exists beyond any contractual arrangement between musician and label.

Crucially, this right is usually 'non-waivable' or 'unassignable', so a rights owner cannot demand artists waive their remuneration right in a contract.

Whenever a recording is exploited in a way that is subject to Performer ER, the artist must be remunerated. Usually it is the licensee's responsibility to ensure remuneration is negotiated and paid, though in some countries (including the UK) the statutory responsibility lies with the copyright owner of the recording.

Copyright law is often silent on what 'equitable remuneration' actually means, though in most countries the label and artist communities have agreed that income generated by the exploitation of the performing rights in sound recordings will be split 50/50 between copyright owners and all performers, and that such remuneration will be deemed 'equitable'.

In most countries the artist community establishes its own CMO (or CMOs — featured artists and session musicians may have their own organisations) which, jointly with the labels' CMO, collects performing rights revenue from licensees and then distributes the money to its members, usually pro-rata based on usage.

In the UK, PPL — although owned by the labels — collects and distributes performing rights income for both labels and artists. Artists become 'performer members' of the society and are paid their share directly. The same is true in the US for featured artists, who receive equitable remuneration for income generated through SoundExchange directly from that body (though session musicians receive their cut via middle-men organisations).

SECTION FIVE:
MONETISING MUSIC RIGHTS BEFORE DIGITAL

5.1 PHYSICAL RECORDINGS

For the latter part of the Twentieth Century the single biggest revenue generator in the music industry was the sale of physical copies of sound recordings (whether pressed to vinyl, cassette, CD or more niche formats).

When selling physical copies in this way, record companies are, in the main, directly exploiting the reproduction rights of their own sound recording copyrights (labels do also license each other's content – mainly for compilations and sample-based tracks – though direct exploitation of copyright is most prevalent).

But the labels do not usually own the copyright in the songs embodied within their recordings, so they are exploiting the reproduction rights of another copyright owner, usually a publisher or a CMO.

They therefore need to secure a reproduction rights licence – what would usually be called a 'mechanical rights licence' – which, for straight cover versions of published songs, is usually provided through the collective licensing system at industry-standard rates (or where a compulsory licence applies possibly at a 'statutory rate', as in the US).

Because labels take all the risk in producing, pressing, distributing and marketing physical releases, it is generally accepted that they should keep the majority of the revenue generated, with the publisher usually receiving less than 10% of the wholesale price of the record.

It's important to note that in the physical market, there is usually just one licensee: the record company. The label exploits its own sound recording copyright and licenses the song copyright. The finished product – the record – is therefore provided to distributor and retailer 'rights ready' so that they do not need to worry about copyright. It is then the responsibility of the record company, which receives from the retailer the wholesale price for each record sold, to account to the publishing sector's mechanical rights CMO.

ROYALTIES

The label then needs to pay a royalty to the featured artist (and any other beneficiaries) according to the terms of each artist's record contract.

Every record contract is different, though an average artist with an average record contract would probably expect to see about 15% of record sales income, though that 15% may be calculated after various other costs have been deducted from monies received by the label. Distributor deals and some independent label contracts may be more generous, while old record contracts from the mid-Twentieth Century will likely be less generous.

How the songwriter is paid, after the label has accounted to and paid the publishing sector's CMO, varies from country to country. In continental Europe, 50% of the money paid by the label to the CMO (or possibly more) would be directly distributed to the songwriter (possibly subject to recoupment). Elsewhere, all monies

Licensing CDs

HOW MUSIC RIGHTS ARE LICENSED FOR PHYSICAL RELEASES LIKE CD AND VINYL

WHICH RIGHTS? | RECORDING RIGHTS | PUBLISHING RIGHTS

WHICH CONTROLS? | REPRODUCTION RIGHTS

RECORDING RIGHTS

Record label exploits its own copyright controls

Label gets licence from and pays revenue share to CMO

PUBLISHING RIGHTS

Publisher (or songwriter) appoints CMO to manage these controls

LABEL IS PAID WHOLESALE PRICE OF CD

CMO IS PAID BLANKET OR COMPULSORY LICENCE RATE (USUALLY % OF WHOLESALE PRICE)

Label pays revenue share to featured artist according to contract

CMO pays all income minus commission to publisher which pays revenue share to songwriters according to contract

OR

CMO pays split of income direct to publisher and songwriter

Licensing radio

HOW MUSIC RIGHTS ARE LICENSED TO CONVENTIONAL RADIO STATIONS

LICENSING OF RADIO IN MOST COUNTRIES

| WHICH RIGHTS? | RECORDING RIGHTS | PUBLISHING RIGHTS | | WHICH CONTROLS? | PERFORMING RIGHTS |

RECORDING RIGHTS

PERFORMER ER IS PAID

| Labels license via their CMO* | Artists license via their CMO* |

CMO IS PAID BLANKET LICENCE RATE

CMO pays label minus commission

CMO pays featured artists and sessions musicians minus commission

PUBLISHING RIGHTS

Songwriters and publishers license via their CMO

CMO IS PAID BLANKET LICENCE RATE

CMO pays 50% to publisher minus commission†

CMO pays 50% to songwriter minus commission

LICENSING OF RADIO IN THE US

| WHICH RIGHTS? | PUBLISHING RIGHTS | | WHICH CONTROLS? | PERFORMING RIGHTS |

RECORDING RIGHTS

PUBLISHING RIGHTS

Songwriters and publishers license via their CMO

CMO IS PAID BLANKET LICENCE RATE

CMO pays 50% to publisher minus commission†

CMO pays 50% to songwriter minus commission

* In the UK the labels and artists use the same CMO, ie PPL
† Publisher may then pass additional cut to songwriter depending on publishing contract

paid by the label would be distributed to the publisher, which would then share that income with their songwriters according to contract.

5.2 BROADCASTING AND LIVE PERFORMANCE

The other key revenue stream for the pre-digital music rights sector – and especially for the music publishers – was income generated through the sale of licenses to companies and individuals (though mainly companies) that wanted to perform or communicate songs or recordings. Broadcasters and concert promoters are the big clients here, though any individual or business playing or performing music in public needs a licence.

As noted above, this is the area where both the record industry and the publishing sector has relied heavily on collective licensing, with rights owners appointing CMOs to issue licences and collect royalties, which are then passed on, minus admin fees, to the labels, publishers, songwriters and artists based (in theory at least) on how often their works were played by licensees.

With regard to the song copyright – where performing and reproduction rights are often split – it is principally the CMOs which control the former that operate in this domain, because licensees are primarily looking to exploit either the performance or communication control. Though

where a licensee also needs to make a copy of a recording before playing it – so a radio station needs to copy tracks to its server – the reproduction rights CMO may also issue a licence.

How CMOs charge for broadcast and performance licences varies according to usage, with fee-per-licence, fee-per-play, annual-lump-sum and revenue share arrangements all regularly employed. More lucrative licensees – including commercial broadcasters and concert promoters – will usually be on revenue share arrangements, so that rights owners benefit as the licensee's business grows.

ROYALTIES

Unlike with record sales, broadcast and performance income is often split more equally between the two sets of music rights[19]. Once money has been allocated between the recording and song copyrights, it must then be split between labels, publishers, artists and songwriters.

On the publishing side, by convention, the CMO will commonly pay 50% direct to publisher and 50% direct to songwriter. On the recordings side, this is where Performer ER often applies, so by convention 50% of income goes to the labels via their CMO and 50% to the artists via their society or societies (as mentioned above, in the UK PPL handles both the label and artist share).

MONETISING MUSIC RIGHTS BEFORE DIGITAL

19: Where it is a recording of a song that is being communicated or performed. Obviously where it is a live performance of a song, so no recording is exploited, only the owner of the song copyright earns any royalties.

This means that broadcast and performance revenue is the one area where income is often more or less split four ways between the labels, publishers, artists and songwriters.

An important exception here is the US, where under federal law there is no 'general' performance or communication control as part of the sound recording copyright[20]. This was the result of a deal between the record industry and the radio sector (which was keen to keep its royalty payments down) when the labels first lobbied Congress for a federal sound recording copyright in the late 1960s, and was based on the argument that radio was an important promotional channel for record companies.

The labels have actually been calling for a general performing right pretty much ever since[21], but so far without success, meaning labels and artists earn nothing when recordings are played on AM/FM radio or in public spaces within the US. Owners of song copyrights do enjoy a general performance control, however, and so license broadcasters, concert promoters and other users of music in the same way as their counterparts elsewhere in the world.

As an aside, federal copyright law only applies to sound recordings released since 1972, with older recordings protected by state-level copyright law. These copyright systems are generally unclear on whether or not performance and communication controls exist for sound recordings. This ambiguity has been the subject of various lawsuits in recent years.

For a time courts in both California and New York ruled there was, in fact, a performance control for recordings under those state's copyright laws. That would basically mean pre-1972 sound recordings enjoy more copyright protection than post-1972 recordings. A more recent judgement in New York concluded there was no general performance control there after all. A final decision is still pending in California, where a relevant case is currently going through appeal.

The US Copyright Office and a number of politicians in US Congress have proposed that federal law should be extended to all sound recordings which would end the ongoing debate over the possiblity of a performance control for recordings existing at a state level.

5.3 SYNCHRONISATION

The third pre-digital revenue stream of note is sync, where film, TV, advert or video game producers wish to 'synchronise' existing songs and/or recordings to moving images.

As with broadcast and performance, this was traditionally a bigger deal revenue stream for publishers than labels, though the record industry has stepped up its efforts in the sync market considerably since CD sales peaked in the late 1990s.

20: There is a specific digital performing right, more on which later.

21: This campaign is currently focused on the proposed Fair Play, Fair Pay Act.

Licensing sync

HOW MUSIC RIGHTS ARE LICENSED FOR SYNC INTO MOVIES OR ADVERTS

WHICH RIGHTS? | RECORDING RIGHTS | PUBLISHING RIGHTS

WHICH CONTROLS? | REPRODUCTION RIGHTS | PERFORMING RIGHTS

RECORDING RIGHTS

Label provides licence for recording rights

Likely referred to as 'master rights' by licensee

LABEL IS PAID SYNC FEE AGREED IN BESPOKE DEAL

Label pays revenue share to featured artist according to contract

PUBLISHING RIGHTS

Publishers license reproduction right directly

Likely referred to as 'sync rights' by licensee

CMO licenses performing right for each broadcast / screening etc

PUBLISHER IS PAID SYNC FEE AGREED IN BESPOKE DEAL

Publisher pays royalty to songwriter according to publishing contract

CMO IS PAID BLANKET LICENCE RATE

CMO pays at least 50% to songwriter and rest to publisher minus commission[†]

† Publisher may then pass additional cut to songwriter depending on publishing contract

Licensing
TV sync

HOW MUSIC RIGHTS ARE LICENSED FOR TV SYNC (UK MODEL VIA CMOs)

WHICH RIGHTS? | RECORDING RIGHTS | PUBLISHING RIGHTS

WHICH CONTROLS? | REPRODUCTION RIGHTS | PERFORMING RIGHTS

RECORDING RIGHTS

PERFORMER ER IS PAID

The labels license TV sync through their CMO (PPL)

CMO IS PAID BLANKET LICENCE RATE

CMO pays label minus commission

CMO pays featured artists and sessions musicians minus commission

PUBLISHING RIGHTS

Publishers and songwriters license TV sync through their CMOs*

Reproduction rights via MCPS | Performing rights via PRS

Both managed via PRS For Music

CMOs ARE PAID BLANKET LICENCE RATE

MCPS pays 100% of royalties to publisher minus commission

Publisher then shares income with songwriter subject to contract

PRS pays 50% to songwriter and 50% to publisher minus commission†

* A small number of songwriters and pubishers do not actually participate in the TV sync blanket licence
† Publisher may then pass additional cut to songwriter depending on publishing contract

Obviously a sync licensee must secure licenses from all and any rights owners who have a stake in the song and/or recording they wish to use. Sync licensing normally begins with direct deals, though TV sync is done via CMOs and blanket licences in many countries.

Broadly, where a copyright is co-owned, any one rights owner can usually refuse to license, scuppering the deal. Under US copyright law, any one rights owner actually has the power to agree a deal for all, providing the other parties are paid their share pro-rata, though industry courtesy and contractual agreements between collaborating songwriters often prevent this.

A sync licensee often needs to exploit both the reproduction and the performing right elements of the copyright. The former when they actually sync the audio to video (which constitutes a reproduction of the work) and the latter whenever the video is broadcast or played in public (which constitutes either a performance or a communication).

The reproduction rights part of the deal is done first directly with the publisher and the label (except where blanket licences are available for TV sync). The sync industry usually refers to the rights being licensed through these deals as the 'synchronisation rights' on the publishing side and the 'master rights' on the recordings side.

The performing rights element may also be part of that initial deal, or – more commonly on the publishing side – will be paid via the collective licensing system each time the finished work that contains the synced music is broadcast or performed, with additional royalties due according to the relevant CMO licence in addition to any fee paid under the original synchronisation deal.

These additional performing rights royalties, where they apply, will usually be factored into the negotiations around the initial sync deal. This cuts both ways. For example, if the final product is to be aired or screened in a market where the collection and distribution of performing rights income is ineffective, the rights owner may seek a premium in the original deal around the reproduction rights.

Where a sync licensee is negotiating directly with multiple rights owners, in theory each deal is separate and subject to its own terms. Though rights owners will often use so called 'most favoured nation' clauses to ensure that all stakeholders in a song and recording earn the same fees for the sync (pro-rata to their stake in the copyright). These clauses mean that whichever rights owner does the deal first could see the fees agreed increase, if another stakeholder subsequently negotiates more favourable terms.

This also often means that the owners of the sound recording copyright and the song copyright will see more or less the same income from any sync deal involving a recording of a song, unless the song is much more famous than the recording. Though, in theory at least, the publisher does generally have a stronger negotiating hand in sync deals, because it is much easier for a licensee to re-record a song than it is to re-write it.

ROYALTIES

The value of sync deals can vary enormously, depending on the budgets of the licensee, the prestige of the songs and recordings being licensed, and quite when and how the music is being used.

Once a deal is done, the publisher and label must then share any income with songwriters and artists according to the terms of their contracts.

As a general rule, under record contracts artists will receive a significantly bigger share of sync than record sale income, commonly 50%.

On the publishing side, any additional performing rights income subsequently collected by the CMOs will be split between publishers and songwriters in the usual way.

5.4 OTHER REVENUES

Other pre-digital revenue streams for music rights owners include:

▶ Selling and licensing sheet music.

▶ Licensing covermount and promotional CDs.

▶ Licensing music and lyrics to karaoke services.

▶ Licensing CD rental services including libraries.

▶ Non-commercial licensing, eg individuals or not-for-profits pressing short run CDs of concerts.

SECTION SIX:
DIGITAL LICENSING

The evolution of the world wide web and the growth of internet access in the 1990s presented both challenges and opportunities for the music industry. While the challenges of piracy have been well documented, other challenges related to legitimate digital platforms: how to license these services, on what terms, and how to process data and royalties. Not all these challenges have, as yet, been fully met.

6.1 WEBCASTS

The first digital services that required licences were online radio stations, ie online services that pretty much replicate traditional radio (and, indeed, are often simulcasts of services already going out on AM or FM).

As webcasts are similar to broadcasts, both the record industry and the publishing sector often opted to license these services through the collective licensing system, ie as with traditional radio. Also following the broadcast model, royalties were often split more or less equally between the recording and publishing rights (the US being the exception here, more on which below).

From a copyright perspective, the main difference between online and traditional radio is that when content is delivered digitally the broadcaster actually exploits both the reproduction and communication controls of the copyright, whereas traditional broadcast only exploits

the communication control. Which is to say that as content is delivered digitally, both copying and a communication occur. (A reproduction may also take place if a conventional radio station copies tracks onto its servers – and this process needs to be licensed – but the broadcast itself only involves a communication to the public).

WEBCASTS AND PUBLISHING RIGHTS

This is particularly important on the publishing side of course, because traditionally reproduction and performing rights are dealt with separately. As webcasters would rather not have to seek two separate licences – one for reproduction rights, one for performing rights – often the publishing industry has sought to provide joint licences, with reproduction and performing right CMOs – where separate – collaborating.

Again the US is different here, in that the big performing rights organisations do not get involved in the licensing of reproduction rights, and ASCAP is not allowed to under the so called 'consent decree' that regulates its operations. Though in the US webcasts have generally been defined as only exploiting the performing rights anyway.

Either way, when joint licences are provided, a decision needs to be made as to how monies paid by a webcaster should be split between the reproduction and performing right elements of the copyright.

This may seem like a mere technicality, given that the ultimate beneficiaries are the same, though in countries where songwriters receive their share of performing right income directly from their CMO but their cut of reproduction right monies via their publisher, the distinction is important. Especially if the songwriter hasn't recouped on their publishing contract, so income coming in from the publisher is set against their advance rather than paid to the writer.

How webcasting income is divided between the reproduction and the performing rights varies from country to country, and is decided by the industry – often via their CMOs – because copyright law provides no guidance on what this split should be.

A common split for webcasts is 75% performing rights and 25% reproduction rights. Though that said, as noted in relation to the US above, in some countries some webcasts – especially simulcasts of AM or FM

radio services – may be treated as only exploiting the performing right, even if – technically speaking – some copying is also taking place.

For example, in July 2015 the BBC decided it could no longer play songs by a handful of writers who are not members of the UK's reproduction rights society MCPS, because a new caching function for offline listening within its smartphone app meant a reproduction rights licence would be required. Which suggests all the other webcasting services already offered by the BBC, but without caching, were entirely covered by its performing rights licence from PRS.

WEBCASTS AND RECORDING RIGHTS

On the sound recordings side, the record labels' CMOs are empowered to license both the reproduction and performing elements of the copyright to webcasters. Technically Performer ER is only due on the performing right element, though artists may still receive 50% of total income. That said, Performer ER rules for webcasts do vary from country to country.

A key difference on the sound recordings side here is the US. As mentioned above, under federal copyright law there is no general performance control with the sound recording copyright. However, a specific digital performance control was added into federal law by new legislation in the 1990s, meaning that while conventional broadcasters are not obliged to secure a licence from sound recording rights owners, webcasters are.

But the same legislation included a compulsory licence for non-interactive webcasting services, meaning that sound recording rights owners are obliged to license webcasters through the collective licensing system. As the US record industry did not have an existing CMO to license traditional broadcasters (it not having previously needed one), SoundExchange was set up to administer this compulsory license, with the rates ultimately set by America's Copyright Royalty Board.

It is worth noting that while sound recording rights owners are obliged to license webcasters in the US through SoundExchange at statutory rates, licensees can opt to negotiate deals directly with the record companies if they so wish. Rights owners might be willing to do such deals if a webcaster provides marketing benefits in addition to royalty payments.

As for how artists are paid in the webcasting domain, this new law introduced Performer ER (in certain circumstances) into US copyright for the first time. The concept hadn't existed in America before, mainly because the revenue stream on which Performer ER is customarily paid elsewhere – performing rights income from sound recordings – didn't exist in the US.

The new law that introduced the digital performing right said that Performer ER (set at 50%, as elsewhere) must be paid on this revenue stream, but only when the webcaster is licensed through SoundExchange. This technically means that if a label could persuade a webcaster to license directly it could avoid paying Performer ER, meaning it could offer the webcaster a 25% discount while earning 25% more itself.

That said, few labels have pursued this arrangement, and the major labels have informally committed to always license webcasters through SoundExchange. Labels would still be obliged to share some of this revenue with featured artists under contract anyway, so that the financial benefits of a direct deal may not be so significant. And the majors may also be aware of the PR damage that could be done if they actively circumvented Performer ER in this way.

A final thing to note on webcasting is this: whereas in most countries the licensing of webcasters closely mirrors the licensing of broadcasters – including how royalties are shared between the song and recording rights – in the US there was no existing framework, because in traditional broadcast a licence was only required from the music publishers, so things have evolved differently.

In particular, because the publishing sector's CMOs generally have a revenue share arrangement with webcasters (as they do with broadcasters) whereas SoundExchange often charges a per-play fee, the labels can end up earning considerably more.

6.2 DOWNLOADS

While webcasters were relatively easy to license, given the many similarities with traditional broadcasters, the first big innovation in digital music provided more challenges. This was, of course, downloads sold through a la carte download stores of the iTunes model. Although in many ways the iTunes music store was as close to a real world record store as was possible in the digital domain, there were three important differences from a copyright perspective: labels becoming licensing companies; publishers licensing the retailer instead of the label; and the making available right. We will consider each of these in turn.

a. Labels become licensing companies

With downloads, the labels were no longer directly exploiting their own sound recording copyrights by reproducing their own masters.

Instead they transferred digital copies of their recordings onto the download store's servers, and then gave the download store operator permission to give their customers permission to download, and therefore reproduce, their recordings, on a pay-per-download basis.

The labels, for whom direct exploitation of copyright had always been their primary business, were now following the publishers' lead in becoming first and foremost licensing companies.

b. Publishers license the retailer instead of the label

When the download market first emerged, the publishers decided to have their own licensing relationships with the download stores, whereas with CDs the label handles song licensing and the retailer receives the finished product 'rights ready', never having to worry about copyright matters. There were three main reasons for this.

Firstly, download stores, unlike traditional retailers, were already in the licensing game, because that was the nature of their relationship with the labels. So it wasn't so big an "ask" that they have a licensing relationship with the publishers too.

Secondly, many publishers felt they'd receive payment quicker and get better sales data if they liaised directly with the download store operators, rather than allowing the labels to be middle men.

Thirdly, this way publishers could consider each new digital business, and digital business model, themselves, and weigh up the value of the song rights to that business.

With hindsight, some of the issues faced today, outlined in section eight below, could have been avoided had publishers continued to license labels, and then have the labels provide download stores with a combined licence (a so called 'pass-through licence'). Though many publishers still feel licensing digital platforms directly, rather than via labels, is the better option.

There are some exceptions to this principle. In the US, partly as a result of the compulsory licensing covering mechanicals, a pass-through licence approach was adopted on download stores. And in some emerging markets, most notably India, pass-through licensing was also agreed to by the publishers for logistical reasons.

c. The making available control

As with a webcast, a download arguably exploits both the reproduction right and performing right elements of the copyright, or to be more specific the reproduction control and the communication control. However, the communication control, where defined in copyright law, traditionally related to conventional broadcasting which, while easily extended to webcasting, might not apply to other kinds of digital transmission.

To ensure digital communication of this kind would still be restricted by copyright, and perhaps to distinguish it from the existing controls that covered broadcasting[22], some rights owners lobbied to have a separate control added to copyright law called 'making available'. The making available right was formally introduced in World Intellectual Property Organisation treaties in 1996 and in the European Union in 2001.

This control has two distinct features to it, firstly that the transmission is 'electronic', and secondly that members of the public "may access it from a place and at a time individually chosen by them". Generally treated as a separate control within the music industry, and usually referred to as the 'making available right', making available could be seen as a sub-category of the existing communication control (and it is formally described as such in UK copyright law).

Since becoming part of most copyright systems in the early 2000s, a number of questions have been raised about making available, notably: when, exactly, it applies; whether labels need a specific performer approval to exploit this right; and the impact of making available on Performer ER. All of these will be dealt with in section eight.

DOWNLOADS AND RECORDING RIGHTS

From the outset, the record industry decided to license download stores directly, while the music publishers inititally opted to license collectively. The record industry opted for direct licensing mainly because a la carte download stores were generally seen as the digital equivalent of the CD market, and labels had always had direct control over their content when it came to physical products, while publishers licensed CDs through their CMOs.

Also, while iTunes initially forced standardised pricing on all rights owners, the labels successfully

22: Which could be subject to compulsory licences.

Licensing downloads

WHICH RIGHTS? RECORDING RIGHTS | PUBLISHING RIGHTS

WHICH CONTROLS? REPRODUCTION RIGHTS | PERFORMING RIGHTS

RECORDING RIGHTS

Label provides licence for recording rights

Treats performing right element as making available

LABEL RECEIVES WHOLESALE PRICE OF DOWNLOAD

Label pays revenue share to featured artist according to contract

PUBLISHING RIGHTS

Reproduction rights licensed either...
Directly by publisher
OR by CMO

Performing rights licensed by CMO (though possibly via JV with publisher)

CMOs ARE PAID BLANKET OR COMPULSORY LICENCE RATE (USUALLY % OF WHOLESALE PRICE)

CMO may pay 50% to writer direct
OR
Publisher collects 100% and pays revenue share to songwriter according to contract

CMO pays at least 50% to songwriter and rest to publisher minus commission†

* In the US a download is treated as only exploiting the reproduction rights
† Publisher may then pass additional cut to songwriter depending on publishing contract

Licensing personalised radio

WHICH RIGHTS? | RECORDING RIGHTS | PUBLISHING RIGHTS

WHICH CONTROLS? | PERFORMING RIGHTS

RECORDING RIGHTS

PERFORMER ER IS PAID*

Available under compulsory licence via SoundExchange

Though DSP can choose to negotiate direct with label if it wishes

PUBLISHING RIGHTS

Songwriters + publishers license via CMOs

DSP can choose to negotiate direct with publisher if it wishes – though publisher can't currently force direct deal under current ASCAP/BMI consent decrees

CMO IS PAID BLANKET LICENCE RATE

CMO IS PAID BLANKET LICENCE RATE

CMO pays label minus commission

CMO pays featured artists and sessions musicians minus commission

CMO pays 50% to publisher minus commission†

CMO pays 50% to songwriter minus commission

* Performer ER technically only applies when service licensed via SoundExchange
† Publisher may then pass additional cut to songwriter depending on publishing contract

persuaded Apple to allow variable pricing controlled by the record company, and that is easier to manage under a direct licensing scenario.

Despite now being in the licensing game – rather than directly exploiting their own copyrights – labels generally treat downloads in much the same way they do CDs, in terms of wholesale pricing and how income is processed. And also in how revenue is shared with featured artists, even where record contracts pre-date iTunes and therefore make no specific provision for the download business. This has proven contentious in the artist community, as we will discuss in section eight.

DOWNLOADS AND PUBLISHING RIGHTS

As with webcasting, the publishers generally provide licences for downloads through their CMOs, though there is now some direct licensing, which we will describe when discussing on-demand streaming below. These licences often cover both the reproduction and performing right elements of the copyright, even when the two sets of rights are ultimately controlled by different parties (except in the US, where a download is treated as just a reproduction). Where you have joint licences, income again needs to be split between the reproduction and performing rights as it is processed. Songwriters would receive their 50% of the performing rights revenue direct from their CMO, while their share of reproduction rights revenue would either be paid direct or via

their publisher, depending on the rules of their local society.

6.3 PERSONALISED RADIO

While download stores were still in their infancy in the early 2000s, a number of start-ups began experimenting with a form of webcasting where content is personalised for each user, rather than radio-style webcasting where all users hear the same content to which they can simple tune in or tune out. Commonly referred to as personalised radio services, the most famous of these platforms today is probably Pandora.

PERSONALISED RADIO AND RECORDING RIGHTS

In the US, the question was quickly raised as to whether or not personalised radio services could license the sound recording rights through SoundExchange, under the same compulsory licence used by more conventional webcasters. If so, the labels – which were still nervous of innovative digital business models at this point – would be obliged to license these services, and the service providers would pay rates ultimately set by the Copyright Royalty Board.

The compulsory licence introduced in the 1990s was arguably intended for more conventional webcasting, to ensure the labels didn't block the growth of standard online radio, and Congress certainly didn't envisage that this licence would apply to fully interactive streaming services like

Spotify. However, the operators of some personalised radio platforms argued that their services were not, in fact, properly interactive so the compulsory licence should apply.

With the law that provided the compulsory licence not conclusive on this point, Yahoo, which had acquired a personalised radio service called Launch, tested the reach of the compulsory licence in court and won, confirming that services of this kind could indeed operate under a SoundExchange licence, paying royalties at rates set by the CRB.

With the publishers also licensing these fledgling companies through the collective licensing system, this made it much easier for such services to legally launch in the US, which is why the personalised radio market grew so early and so quickly there, and why this kind of streaming service, and especially Pandora and iHeartRadio, remain so significant in the country, despite fully on-demand streaming dominating in Europe.

It is important to note that music rights owners came to resent the way Pandora was licensed, especially after the company's IPO made its founders rich and its finances public. Subsequent and seemingly relentless efforts by the digital company to persuade the CRB and the collective licensing courts to reduce its royalty payments exacerbated that resentment.

Though relations have improved in more recent years and, actually, both Pandora and iHeartRadio have now

agreed direct deals with many of the record companies, even though they are entitled to license recordings through SoundExchange if they so wish. Under the compulsory licence, rights owners are obliged to offer a licence via their society, but licensees aren't obliged to use that system and can try to negotiate direct deals.

PERSONALISED RADIO AND PUBLISHING RIGHTS

Before Pandora and iHeartRadio started voluntariy doing direct deals with the labels – and while the company was busy trying to force its royalty commitments down through the CRB and the courts – some of the big music publishers in the US attempted to force the former into direct deals, believing they could secure better rates that way.

Unlike with recordings, there wasn't actually a compulsory licence obliging the publishers to license their performing rights to services like Pandora, though the main performing rights organisations – ASCAP and BMI – were obliged to offer a licence. But what if the publishers pulled their digital rights out of the PROs, so that Pandora had to do a direct deal?

Except, they couldn't. When some publishers announced they would pull their digital rights out of the PROs, Pandora challenged that decision in the courts, successfully arguing that the so called 'consent decrees' that regulate BMI and ASCAP forbid partial withdrawal of rights from societies (partial withdrawal of this kind is possible at the European societies, albeit only with songwriter consent).

This meant that to force Pandora into direct deals the publishers would need to start licensing all customers of their performing rights – including AM/FM radio stations and concert promoters – directly, a move that would pose both logistical and legal challenges.

The publishers were not happy with this decision. To that end they successfully lobbied the US Department Of Justice – which oversees the consent decrees – to review how ASCAP and BMI were regulated. But, despite initial indications that that review would likely result in changes to allow partial withdrawal, in the end the DoJ declined to amend the consent decrees.

Had the consent decrees been altered to allow partial withdrawal, while that would have pleased the big music publishers, it would also have posed a number of questions and challenges.

First, can US publishers simply withdraw the digital performing rights of their songs from ASCAP and BMI without explicit permission from songwriters?

And, with international repertoire, which is licensed by ASCAP and BMI through their reciprocal agreements with other CMOs around the world – which often exclusively mandate the US societies to act as licensors – withdrawal would not be have been possible without the approval and, likely, the participation of those societies. How would that work?

As with the recording rights, Pandora did subsequently voluntarily agree some direct deals with the music publishers, despite them still having the option to also license via ASCAP and BMI (in the US, unlike elsewhere, publishers and licensees can circumvent the CMOs when licensing performing rights if all parties agreed to the direct deal).

PERSONALISED RADIO OUTSIDE THE US

Outside the US there are fewer personalised radio services, and those that have launched have not always gained traction on the same level as Spotify-style platforms.

Outside the US labels may license personalised radio services directly, though in some countries they may also allow their CMOs to license services where SoundExchange would license in the US, even though they are not obliged to under law. Where they have done so, Performer ER may or may not be paid depending on local conventions.

Publishers outside the US also initially licensed these services through CMOs in a similar way to more conventional webcasts, though some repertoire may now be licensed directly in the way we will outline in the next section.

In the US, as with webcasts, it was deemnd that personalised radio only actually exploited the peforming rights, even though technically copying is also occuring. But elsewhere personalised radio royalties may still be split between

Licensing streams

HOW MUSIC RIGHTS ARE LICENSED TO ON-DEMAND STREAMING PLATFORMS

WHICH RIGHTS? | RECORDING RIGHTS | PUBLISHING RIGHTS

WHICH CONTROLS? | REPRODUCTION RIGHTS | PERFORMING RIGHTS

RECORDING RIGHTS

Label provides licence for recording rights

Treats performing right element as making available

LABEL PAID REVENUE SHARE BASED ON CONSUMPTION SHARE (OR MINIMUM RATE)

Label pays revenue share to featured artist according to contract

PUBLISHING RIGHTS

Reproduction rights licensed either...
Directly by publisher
OR by CMO

Performing rights licensed by CMO (though possibly via JV with publisher)

CMOs PAID REVENUE SHARE BASED ON CONSUMPTION SHARE (OR MINIMUM RATE)

CMO may pay 50% to writer direct
OR
Publisher collects 100% and pays revenue share to songwriter according to contract

CMO pays at least 50% to songwriter and rest to publisher minus commission[†]

† Publisher may then pass additional cut to songwriter depending on publishing contract

the reproduction and performing rights, which may affect how songwriters are paid.

6.4 ON-DEMAND STREAMING

The biggest growth area in recorded music today (and for a few years now) is fully on-demand streaming, so digital service providers (DSPs) like Spotify, Apple Music, Deezer, Tidal, Google Play Music, Napster and Amazon Music Unlimited. In the US, Pandora and iHeartRadio also now offer this kind of streaming in addition to personalised radio.

These services first began to emerge around 2006 (though some DSPs existed earlier with different models), and really took off after 2008, when the record companies – and particularly the majors – seemed to have a change of heart regarding digital, and started to more proactively investigate and consider new approaches to monetising their content, albeit providing the DSPs agreed to some sizable upfront demands.

ON-DEMAND STREAMING AND RECORDING RIGHTS

With the SoundExchange compulsory licence in the US definitely not applying to these services, the record industry worldwide opted to license fully on-demand streaming platforms directly, though most indies either rely on digital rights body Merlin to negotiate their deals or they piggy-back on a distributor's existing arrangement.

Fully on-demand streaming services, whether advertising or subscription funded, required a very different approach to licensing on the labels' part. Unlike the CD and download market, where the labels charge a set wholesale price per sale to the retailer or download store, streaming services are usually licensed on a revenue share basis, similar to the way performing rights organisations often license bigger concert promoters and broadcasters.

That said, because when a streaming service first launches there is very little revenue in which to share, and because some DSPs will fail before generating any serious income, the labels build in a number of contingencies, meaning these deals have up to five components.

▶ Firstly, there will be the core revenue share element. Labels generally seek 50-60% of any revenue generated by the DSP that can be allocated to their recordings.

▶ Secondly, there will be a series of minima guarantees for the label, which means that whatever revenues a DSP generates, the label will receive a minimum sum of money each time one of their tracks is streamed, and possibly for each subscriber the DSP signs up as well.

▶ Thirdly, there will be an upfront cash advance, so whatever happens the label knows it will make a minimum sum of money in any one licensing period. Further royalty payments by the DSP begin once the advance has been recouped.

▶ Fourthly, with start-ups the labels

will usually demand equity in the company, aware that the single biggest revenue generator may be the sale of the streaming business, either to an existing major tech or media firm or through flotation on a stock exchange (IPO).

▶ Fifthly, on first deal labels may add an admin or technology fee to cover the costs of providing and ingesting content to the DSP's specific requirements.

Where a DSP has both an ad funded and subscription level, and things like student discounts and family packages, and partnerships that bundle paid-for subscriptions in with a mobile, ISP or other third party service, the label will likely negotiate a separate deal for each option. Each month revenue and usage data will need to be provided, and royalties calculated, separately for each part of the deal

Once the deal is in place, each month (or thereabouts) the DSP will report to the label for the period just gone all of the information shown below...

The DSP then calculates what proportion of overall revenue could be attributed to the label's recordings, based on the proportion of the total number of streams that came from the record company's catalogue (so B divided by E). It then pays the label 50-60% of that money depending on the terms of its specific deal.

Unless, that is, the minimum rate for the total number of streams (so D multiplied by the per-play minimum rate) – or indeed any other minima that has been guaranteed – is higher, in which case the DSP pays that sum to the label instead.

In theory, as a streaming service matures, most elements of the original deal should become irrelevant. Equity and admin fees will probably only be demanded on first deal, and as a service becomes successful – so that monthly revenues always exceed minimum payments – the minima should become irrelevant too (though ad-funded services may always be at the

A	Total number of subscribers.
B	Total revenues after sales tax has been deducted.
C	Total number of streams.
D	Total number of streams from the label's catalogue.
E	Proportion of total streams that came from the label's catalogue (so C divided by D).

How royalties are calculated

1 Calculate Revenue

Net revenue of DSP

÷

Total tracks streamed by DSP

X

Label's % of consumption

= £X

2 Calculate Share

£X

X

Share % agreed

= £Y

3 Final Payment

Is £Y greater than the minimum per play rate?

YES   NO

Revenue share £Y paid

Minimum per play rate paid

whim of the advertising market, so revenues will fluctuate).

As an aside, it is worth noting that while this is the current model employed by streaming services, an alternative has been proposed, where each individual subscriber's subscription fee is divided pro-rata between the rights owners of the songs and recordings that specific subscriber played in any one month. This would mean the per-play rate would vary greatly depending on how many tracks the subsciber streamed in any one month.

Some DSPs and labels have actively considered this alternative 'user-centric' approach to streaming royalties, though none of the big streaming services have as yet adopted it. Doing so would require permission from the rights owners.

However the royalties due are calculated at the DSP, once the labels have been paid, they must then share the income with featured artists according to their record contracts. As with downloads, most labels have based the artist's share of streaming income on the splits they already received on CD sales (either explicitly in new contracts or by interpreting pre-digital contracts in this way), which is usually a relatively low split (commonly 15%, maybe a few percent more for streams).

As with downloads this has proven controversial, and indeed even more so, because many artists feel that the label's costs and risks are reduced in the streaming domain. There is also an argument that, because streaming arguably exploits performing rights more than reproduction rights, Performer ER should be paid on some of this income.

However, the labels argue that the performing right element of streaming constitutes 'making available' rather than straight 'communication to the public', and that Performer ER does not apply when that is the case. Both these arguments are contentious and we will return to them in section eight below.

ON-DEMAND STREAMING AND PUBLISHING RIGHTS

On the publishing side of streaming, the distinction between reproduction and performing rights becomes important once again, as does the role of the CMOs. While the publishing sector initially licensed streaming services collectively, in some other markets, and especially Europe, the big publishers now license some repertoire – principally Anglo-American repertoire[23] – directly.

a. Direct licensing
However, this move to direct licensing posed a challenge because – as discussed above – outside the US the publishers do not control song copyrights outright, rather the songwriter assigns (basically) some elements of the copyright to their CMO instead. The publisher then

23: The definition of 'Anglo-American repertoire' can vary, though commonly includes songs registered with CMOs in UK, Ireland, US, Canada, Australia and South Africa.

How recording royalties flow

ON-DEMAND STREAMING SERVICE

MAJORS & THEIR DISTRIBUTORS	INDIES VIA MERLIN	INDIES VIA DISTRIBUTORS*	ARTISTS VIA DISTRIBUTORS*

SONY MUSIC

UNIVERSAL

The Orchard

ada
ALTERNATIVE DISTRIBUTION ALLIANCE • INDEPENDENT

caroline

MERLIN

believe.

(i)INgrooves
MUSIC GROUP

idol

FUGA

tuneCORE

DI++O

DISTROKID

cdbaby

RECORD LABEL

ARTIST

*There are obviously many distributors, a few examples are shown here

How song royalties flow

HOW MONEY COMMONLY FLOWS FROM DSP TO SONGWRITERS

ON-DEMAND STREAMING SERVICE

THE BIG FIVE
(ANGLO-AMERICAN REPERTOIRE)

OTHER REPERTOIRE
VIA CMOS & THEIR HUBS*

BMG   K

Sony/ATV
MUSIC PUBLISHING

WARNER/CHAPPELL

UNIVERSAL

PERFORMING RIGHTS

sacem

SOCAN

PRS for Music

MECHANICAL RIGHTS

sacem

CMRRA

mcps

PERFORMING RIGHT ROYALTIES FLOW VIA CMO

MECHANICAL RIGHT ROYALTIES FLOW DIRECT SUBJECT TO CONTRACT

PUBLISHER

SONGWRITER

*There are obviously many CMOs, a few examples are shown here enjoys just a contractual share of the revenue generated by those elements of the copyright. This means that, whereas the record companies can easily cut their CMOs out of the deal making process, the music publishers do not have that power, especially if the licensee needs to exploit both performing and reproduction rights.

Nevertheless, as the digital market matured the big music publishers in Europe decided they wanted to start licensing some digital services directly, arguing that this would benefit both corporate rights owners and songwriters if it resulted in higher royalties overall, while digital service providers would also benefit, because direct deals could usually be completed quicker and on a multi-territory basis[24].

The big publishers were confident direct dealing would result in better rates, not least because direct deals would not be subject to collective licensing regulation, strengthening their negotiating hand. And, unlike in the US, European collective licensing rules (formulated in response to a line of cases from the Court Of Justice Of The European Union) said that publishers could exercise so called 'partial withdrawal' and license digital directly while continuing to license other sets of users, like radio and concert promoters, though the collective licensing system.

However, because the CMOs actually control some of the elements of

the copyright that the DSPs seek to exploit, the publishers couldn't simply start licensing direct on their own. So instead they each formed joint ventures with one or another European society, called 'special purpose vehicles', or SPVs.

Each of these ventures was then empowered to represent the reproduction rights in its parent publisher's Anglo-American catalogue, and would then gain permission from relevant CMOs to also represent the performing rights of the same songs. This means the SPV can then negotiate a direct deal with each DSP that covers all elements of songs in the publisher's repertoire. The deal making is led by the publisher, but terms must be approved by participating CMOs.

Publishers which have gone this route are:

▶ **Sony/ATV/EMI** via SOLAR, a joint venture (JV) with PRS and GEMA.

▶ **Universal Music Publishing** via DEAL, a JV with SACEM.

▶ **Warner/Chappell** via PEDL, a JV with various societies but mainly PRS.

▶ **BMG** via ARESA, a JV with GEMA.

▶ **Kobalt** originally via a JV with STIM, and now via AMRA, the society Kobalt bought but which continues to operate as an autonomous body.

▶ Some of the bigger indies are now moving in this direction via the IMPEL initiative, which works with PRS.

24: Some CMOs do now offer multi-territory licences and this trend is growing, though licensing in that way is arguably simpler with direct dealing.

As with other digital licences, once streaming revenue is received it is split between the performing and reproduction rights (splits vary from country to country). Once collected and split between the two sets of rights, income then works its way through the system, some going direct to the publisher, some through the CMO, with the songwriter again possibly receiving their share from two sources, ie from both publisher and society.

b. Collective licensing

Of course, while the five publishers now negotiating digital deals direct control a lot of repertoire, they do not control it all, and the direct deals only generally cover Anglo-American catalogue. And whereas on the recordings side, where if a DSP doesn't have a deal in place with a smaller rights owners it just doesn't carry that label's content, on the publishing side it is more complicated because co-ownership of copyright is so common and ownership data is not always easy to come by.

This means that a DSP may receive a recording from a label, and have deals in place with publishers that control 80% of the song, but not with the one indie publisher which controls the other 20%. In theory the DSP shouldn't stream this recording because it is not fully licensed. But it can be hard for the digital service to know that it hasn't got all the licences it needs in place for that individual song, and even if it is aware of that issue, it probably won't know which independent controls the remaining 20%.

This basically means DSPs need to get licensing deals in place with pretty much every publisher to make things work. This 'mop up' can generally be done through the collective licensing system. So basically a DSP in Europe needs to do deals with SOLAR, DEAL, PEDL, ARESA and AMRA, and then an individual deal with the local collecting society in each and every country in which it wishes to operate (always ensuring that both performing and reproduction rights are covered).

DSPs do not especially like this arrangement and the number of deals that must be done. Though the societies are trying to reduce the total number of deals required by forming 'hubs' that are empowered to offer licences covering the repertoires of multiple societies. In Europe the two key hubs are ICE (mainly representing societies in Northern Europe) and Armonia (mainly representing soceities in Southern Europe).

c. Mechanical rights in the US

In the US there has been a different challenge for DSPs seeking to ensure that they have all song rights covered. On the performing rights side, the DSPs can get blanket licences from the PROs like in Europe (though there are four PROs in the US – the aforementioned ASCAP and BMI plus SESAC and GMR – so four deals are required). But there is no industry wide CMO offering a blanket licence for reproduction rights.

There is a compulsory licence covering mechanical rights in the US – so DSPs know what they must pay – but under the terms of that compulsory licence they must alert a rights owner that their songs are being exploited. This requires the DSP to identify and contact the rights owner. However, they do not automatically know who the rights owner is, or even which specific song is contained within any one recording that a label provides. The label doesn't provide this information (and doesn't necessarily have all the required information anyway) and there is no one-stop central database identifying which songs are contained in which recordings and which writers and publishers control those songs.

There are a number of agencies that can help licensees identify rights owners, the biggest of which is probably The Harry Fox Agency, which used to owned by the National Music Publishers Association. HFA traditionally processed mechanical royalties for record labels, most of which treated the agency as if it was a mechanical rights society like the UK's MCPS.

But these agencies are not CMOs in the true sense and do not offer blanket licences. And in the streaming domain, where licensees need to clear the rights in millions of tracks, some of these agencies have struggled to process all the paperwork required by the compulsory licence. Which means some writers and publishers have not been paid their mechanical royalties. Some of those unpaid writers and publishers have sued the DSPs resulting in multi-million dollar lawsuits.

The DSPs, who are happy to pay mechanical royalties but are unhappy with the work involved in making those payments and the legal ramifications of not being able to identify a rights owner, have been putting pressure on the American music publishers to develop a different licensing system. At one point, in one legal battle, Spotify went as far as questioning whether mechanical royalties were even due on streams, basically suggesting that all streaming income be processed by the performing rights organisations.

To that end, the National Music Publishers Association is now proposing that the compulsory licence for mechanical rights be amended, and that as part of that reform a new CMO be created empowered to offer a blanket licence for mechanical rights in the US, as is available in most other territories. These proposals would require a change to copyright law and are contained in the Music Modernization Act that was proposed in US Congress in December 2017.

d. Deals and data

The publishers' deals – whether directly or collectively negotiated – are similar to those of the labels in that they are ultimately revenue share arrangements, but with some minimum guarantees and an upfront advance. Publishers generally seek 10-15% of any revenue that can be allocated to their songs and payments are calculated in a similar way to with the labels.

Though it is worth noting that co-ownership and the lack of good ownership data creates further challenges here. Because there is no central database identifying who owns and controls each song copyright or – where songs are co-owned – what the respective splits are, the DSPs generally rely on the publishers and CMOs to tell them what they are due based on what songs have been streamed in any one month.

So (except with mechanical royalties in the US), a DSP provides the SPVs and CMOs with a spreadsheet recording every single stream that took place in the preceding month. The SPV and CMO must then identify every stream that exploited a song it controls, and then work out what it is owed based on its revenue share or minima arrangement, and according to what percentage of the song it owns or controls.

This 'back reporting' creates two problems. First, processing that level of data is a massive task. The CMOs are now having to process unprecedented amounts of data,

and the total amount increases each month as the streaming services grow. Many have struggled with this. And second, there are discrepancies between different publisher's and CMO's databases as to who controls what songs, and especially what the percentage splits are in co-owned tracks.

Meaning the DSPs are sometimes asked to pay out more than 100% of the monies due on any one stream. Where this happens digital services usually delay payment until the conflict is resolved, which delays payment to the publisher and songwriter.

It is hoped that the aforementioned CMO hubs – as well as making licensing simpler for the DSPs – can also help tackle these challenges too by pooling the data processing efforts of participating societies and the SPVs they are involved in, and by having one central pool of ownership data so that disputes over splits are less likely to happen. Nevertheless, worldwide these challenges remain.

SECTION SEVEN:
ISSUES & VIEWPOINTS

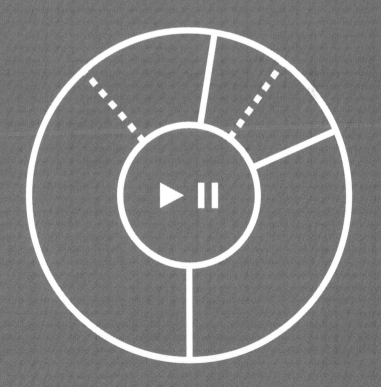

When part one of 'Dissecting The Digital Dollar' was originally published in 2015 it identified a number of issues with the current model. Some of these were issues for the industry at large including the DSPs, some were issues for the music community, and some specifically for artists and songwriters.

In 2016 MMF staged a series of roundtable discussions involving artists, songwriters, labels, publishers, lawyers, accountants and managers. A whole series of these roundtables were staged in the UK, while additional sessions also took place in the US, Canada and France.

An in depth summary of these discussions was published in October 2016, which is still available to download from the MMF website. Based on the roundtables, the MMF also identified a number of action points for itself, the management community and the wider music industry. This has informed the MMF's subsequent lobbying agenda and educational initiatives.

In this section we review the issues raised in the initial 'Dissecting The Digital Dollar' report and summarise both the opinions expressed during the roundtables and the action points the MMF identified.

7.1 DIVISION OF REVENUE

As the primary way recorded music is commercialised has shifted from physical to digital, and more recently from downloads to streams, there has been much debate as to how monies generated by digital services should be divided between the different stakeholders, ie between the digital platforms, labels, publishers, CMOs, artists and songwriters.

Quite how the money is shared varies according to: each deal between a DSP and a rights owners; each artist and songwriter's individual label and publishing contracts; and collecting society conventions. Splits are also evolving because DSP deals are renegotiated every few years and revenue share arrangements have been altered slightly. The diagram on the opposite page shows an approximation of how the digital dollar has been shared – on average – to date.

There are various components to the division of revenue debate.

a. The rights owners / digital platforms split

Question one: How should digital income be split between the music industry and the digital platforms themselves?

Slicing the digital pie

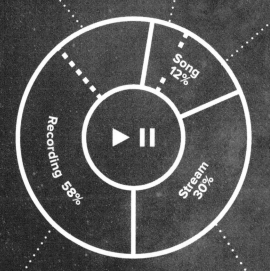

Publisher
3.6%

Artist
11.6%

Songwriter
8.4%

Song
12%

Recording 58%

Stream
30%

Label
46.4%

DSP
30%

*More recent deals may have seen the allocation to recordings slightly decrease and to songs slightly increase.

Most DSPs — both download stores and streaming platforms — see themselves as the new retailers. This meant that, when the early digital services first began negotiating with the record companies, music publishers and CMOs, there was some precedent on which the digital services could base their proposed business models, in that they knew what cut of the pie traditional CD sellers had taken.

This has resulted in most streaming services seeking to keep approximately 30% of their post-sales-tax revenue. Though it is worth noting that this is very much an approximate figure, because each rights owner has a different revenue share arrangement with each streaming service, meaning that the DSP might have to share anywhere between 60% and 75% of the revenue attributed to any one stream. Some streams, therefore, will be more costly than others. Across the board it averages out at about 70%.

Though most deals between rights owners and DSPs put more of the initial risk on the latter, in that the digital service is obliged to make certain minimum payments to the labels and publishers irrespective of revenue, as outlined above. This may not always apply during trial periods that are completely free to the user, but does with ad-funded freemium and post-trial-period premium when the DSP is yet to reach critical mass.

This means that, in the early days, a start-up streaming service will likely be making payments to the

rights owners that exceed their entire revenues. This is why it is an expensive business setting up a new streaming platform. Nevertheless, there are some in the music community who propose that the streaming services should be paying more than 70% of their revenues to the rights owners in the long-term. Though, in the main, the DSPs are unsurprisingly resistant to this proposal.

Indeed, a report published in 2015 by the UK's Entertainment Retailer's Association, which counts the key DSPs amongst its membership, argued that the mainly loss-making streaming services are already struggling to grow their businesses on a 30% split, given the infrastructures they have had to build and the advances and guarantees they have had to pay. The report contained the quote: "70% is tough enough, but at 80%, we would have to shut up shop. Somebody should explain that 80% of nothing is... nothing".

Some DSPs have entered the market by promising to pay slightly higher royalties to the music industry, though in the main most streaming firms remain committed to the 70/30 model. And some expect that in the future DSPs may seek to reduce their overall commitment to the music industry further to ensure profitability.

Most DSPs also now produce some of their own content, generally radio-style programmes and/or live sessions. If the services were to make more of this content — and prioritise it within their apps — they could

DISSECTING THE DIGITAL DOLLAR

probably reduce their commitments to the music industry further.

Some also argue that the DSPs might ultimately start to commission their own music at some point – or start signing artists and, in essence, become labels – in order to further reduce royalty costs. Though it is debatable quite how good that would be as a cost-saving measure, given the risks associated with signing artists, especially new talent.

But DSPs could probably create their own catalogues of music for certain genres, like the music that fills the average service's 'chill-out' and 'relaxation' playlists.

Either way, the music industry demanding that the DSPs take a cut below the 30% average at this point in the streaming sector's evolution is probably optimistic.

FROM THE ROUNDTABLES

With that in mind, participants from all the stakeholder groups represented at the 'Digital Dollar' roundtables generally agreed that it was basically reasonable for the DSPs to aim to keep approximately 30% of their revenue, for now at least.

Some participants also noted that, because of the aforementioned minimum guarantees and advances, few services actually kept 30% of their revenue anyway.

b. The recording rights / publishing rights split

Question two: Of the 65-75% of streaming revenues paid to the music industry, how should these monies be split between the two copyrights, ie the recordings and the songs?

Each rights owner has its own deal with each digital platform and the exact terms of those deals are often secret. But we know that sound recording owners will likely have a revenue share arrangement of around 50-60%, while song owners will likely have a revenue share arrangement of between 10-15%. Which means the label is likely to be taking approximately four to six times more than the publisher.

This disparity is not new. Indeed in the CD domain the label/publisher split would be tipped even more to the former's advantage. There are various reasons for this, including the facts that:

▶ A sound recording copyright owner only earns from their one specific recording of a song, while the publisher earns on every version and variation of the work.

▶ The owner of the song also earns every time the work is performed live, and so also enjoys a cut of the live sector's income.

▶ A sound recording copyright term lasts for a fixed time after release (50-95 years, depending on country), whereas the song term runs for the life of the creator and then a set period of time (commonly 50-70 years depending on country), meaning song copyrights usually last significantly longer than recording copyrights.

But most importantly, the sound recording owner – ie the label – does a lot more work in getting the CD to market. It pays for the recording to be made, for CDs to be pressed and distributed, and for the marketing campaign that will, if successful, result in sales. The publisher, while paying an advance to the songwriter, has none of this risk, and with risk comes reward. Which is principally why the label earned so much more from CD sales than the publisher.

However, when it comes to other uses of recorded music – such as the broadcast or public performance of sound recordings – in the main both rights owners often receive a similar sum of money from licensees (outside the US that is, in America labels actually receive nothing because, as mentioned above, there is only a digital performing right with the sound recording copyright). So, while it may often be down to the label to get new recordings to radio stations and club DJs, the assumption here is that record companies are taking a much lower risk and so the rewards are shared out more equally.

In the main, something akin to the CD model has been applied to both downloads and streams. Even though it could be argued that, while iTunes was the digital evolution of the record shop, Spotify is actually the digital evolution of radio. That logic might suggest a publisher/label split more inline with traditional broadcast, so that any revenues paid to the music industry are split more equally between the two copyrights.

Though few are actually proposing a 50/50 arrangement between the record industry and the music publishing sector on streaming income. And many record companies argue that such an arrangement would almost certainly put them out of business. Because even if there are parallels between Spotify and traditional radio, the labels continue to take a considerable risk when creating new recorded content to pump into the streaming services.

And while the costs of distribution may be considerably less in digital than physical, there are still significant costs associated with creating new recorded music and marketing those releases, while digital rights administration still requires some resource. Labels have also had to digitise their catalogues and invest in systems to get their content onto the digital platforms.

But are the labels really taking as big a risk in the digital age as when they were primarily selling CDs? And won't their risks decline further as digital-only releases become the norm and the initial set-up costs of the industry's shift to digital are paid off? And aren't many labels now partly securing their investments in new talent by taking a cut of revenue streams beyond the sound recording copyright, such as merchandise, live income and brand partnerships?

Some in the music publishing industry are now starting to publicly bemoan the level of income they are receiving from the booming streaming sector, and songwriters in particular have become vocal on this issue in recent years. And while these complaints have been partly aimed at the DSPs themselves, and in the US at the compulsory and collective licensing rules that impact what publishing royalties digital services pay, some have questioned why there is such a disparity between label and publisher payments on streaming music.

Though some in the publishing sector argue that publishers and CMOs should continue to focus on getting the best possible deals for their respective repertoires, rather than getting into a turf war with the labels. But given that most digital platforms license recordings first (indeed some start-up services go live with some publishing deals still pending), the fact that up to 60% of revenue is already committed to the record companies before the DSPs do their deals with the publishers will surely always limit what the digital services can afford to pay for the song rights.

FROM THE ROUNDTABLES

All but the representatives from record companies felt that the way streaming income is currently split between the recording rights and the publishing rights – so that the owners of the former are paid four to six times more than the latter – feels inequitable.

Though few actually advocated a 50/50 split, with most people conceding that labels still took considerable risks when releasing new music, especially from new talent. But it was felt those risks were less significant than in the CD era.

Label representatives argued that their risks were actually as high as ever, despite the fall in recording, manufacture and distribution costs. But few other participants were wholly convinced of that argument.

In addition to the discussion as to whether or not more streaming income should be allocated to the song rights, there is the separate question as to how a repositioning of this split might be achieved.

Altering this split is tricky because the publishers and their CMOs opted to have their own commercial relationships with the DSPs, rather than licensing the labels and letting them provide content to the streaming platforms with all rights covered (remember, in the CD domain, the label not the retailer was the publisher's licensee).

As mentioned above, the main reason for this was that the publishers and their CMOs generally felt that, by having their own separate arrangements with the DSPs, they would get paid faster and would have better access to usage data. With hindsight, there is also an argument that the labels would have been more resistant to the bigger publishers subsequently going the direct licensing route (via their SPV joint ventures with the CMOs), the record companies having generally paid publishers set rates through the collective licensing system in the past.

All these reasons for the publishing sector licensing the DSPs rather than the labels are still sound. But this arrangement means that there is no direct commercial relationship between the labels and the publishers when it comes to digital licensing, leaving the DSP somewhat caught in the middle if the two sides of the music rights industry start to dispute the way digital royalties should be split between the different music copyrights.

Except, of course, many music rights firms – and all of the majors – own both labels and publishers, so there is a commercial link at the top of these businesses. Though music rights companies with interests in both sound recording and song copyrights would likely prefer the status quo – ie the majority of the money coming in through their labels – because generally record companies pay artists a much smaller share of income than publishers do songwriters (and at least some of the publishing income is paid direct to songwriters via the CMOs).

All that said, there has, in fact, been a slight reslicing of the digital pie in terms of the recording rights / publishing rights share. Some publishers have managed to negotiate their revenue share splits up slightly in recent years – ie by a few per cent. Meanwhile the DSPs have pursuaded the labels to take a slight cut, in part to compensate for the publishers' increase. The question is, do songwriters and publishers see an increase of a few per cent as a satisfactory conclusion to this particular issue? Probably not.

Though you sense that the record companies hope that publishers and songwriters will be ulltimately placated down the line as streaming revenues boom and even a minority split of the money becomes lucrative. The record industry is now back in growth on the back of the streaming boom, and publishers and writers are sharing in that boom. Though many, especially writers, still argue that their streaming income is simply not enough.

c. The reproduction rights / performing rights split

Question three: Downloads and streams exploit both the reproduction and communication controls of the copyright – ie both the reproduction and the performing rights. How should income be allocated between the two elements of each copyright?

RECORDING RIGHTS

On the sound recording side, it could be argued that this distinction is an academic one, because the record company routinely controls both elements of the copyright, and artist contracts don't usually distinguish between reproduction and performing rights when it comes to royalties (record contracts are more likely to distinguish between 'sales' and 'licence' income, more on which below).

That said, Performer ER is relevant here. Under most copyright systems Performer ER is due when the performing rights of a sound recording copyright are exploited, but not when the reproduction rights are used. However, Performer ER has not been paid on most digital income to date for reasons outlined below.

But if it were, it would only be due on the performing right allocation of digital revenue, not the reproduction right allocation (where featured artists would instead be due royalties as set out in their label contract), so at that point how digital monies were allocated between the two elements of the copyright would become important to both labels and artists.

PUBLISHING RIGHTS

But the reproduction/performing rights split is already important on the publishing side. This is particulary true in countries where different CMOs have traditionally represented the two sets of rights. But even where one CMO controls both reproduction rights and performing rights, how the songwriter gets paid may differ depending on which are exploited.

Under the UK system, 50% of performing rights income is always paid directly to the songwriter by PRS, oblivious of whether or not they have recouped on their publishing deal. But all reproduction rights income is paid to the publisher (with streaming, either directly or via MCPS), which then pays the songwriter their share according to their specific publishing contract. For signed songwriters, therefore, it will likely be beneficial for more digital income to be allocated to the performing right than the reproduction right (especially if they are yet to recoup on their publishing deal).

Copyright law does not actually define what controls are exploited in a download and stream, nor what the split should be between the two controls. Therefore the industry defines these splits itself.

Generally it has been agreed a download exploits the reproduction rights more than a stream. But exact splits vary from country to country, and have also changed over time. A common split is 75% reproduction / 25% performing for downloads; 25% reproduction / 75% performing for webcasts and personalised radio; and 50/50 for on-demand streams.

But it varies. And, as noted above, in the US a download is treated as only exploiting the reproduction rights and a personalised radio stream just the performing rights. Though, with an on-demand stream, both are exploited.

d. The artist / label split

Question four: Where a record label owns the copyright in a sound recording but pays a royalty to the featured artist under the terms of their record contract, what royalty should the label pay on downloads and streams compared to CDs?

There has been much debate since the early days of iTunes as to how digital income should be shared between labels and artists. There has been much less debate about the similar split between publishers and songwriters, possibly because publishing contracts are traditionally much more generous to songwriters than record contracts are to artists, usually because labels make much bigger upfront investments than publishers[25].

Every contract is different, of course, though publishing contracts will always see the songwriter take at least 50% of revenue and possibly, in more modern contracts, significantly more. On the label side, while some indie label deals may offer a 50/50 net split with the artist, a more common arrangement will see the record company keep the majority of core income streams.

SALES V LICENCE

A convention of record contracts is that the royalties paid by the label to the artist often differ according to revenue stream, so that while the label may keep 85% of record sale monies, a more generous 50/50 arrangement may apply to other income, such as sync. This distinction was often described in pre-digital contracts using the terms 'sale' (where money was generated by directly exploiting the copyright, eg selling CDs) and 'licence' (where money was generated through licensing deals, eg sync).

This has created a problem for record companies with legacy contracts that do not specifically mention downloads or streams because digital is clearly a licensing rather than sales scenario, in that the label gives permission to the digital platform to exploit their copyrights, rather than directly making and selling copies of their recordings. A strict interpretation of a conventional pre-digital record contract, therefore, could require the label to pay the higher 'licence' royalty on all digital income.

In the main this has not happened, with the vast majority of labels paying the lower 'sales' royalty on downloads, and many on streams too. A significant number of veteran artists have sued their record companies on this point of contractual interpretation, albeit mainly in the US.

The landmark case is FBT Productions v Universal Music, relating to the stake producers Mark and Jeff Bass have in the early recordings of Eminem, who is signed to Universal label Interscope. After long-drawn out litigation on the sales v licence point, FBT Productions won the case, subsequently securing a higher royalty on digital income stemming from the Eminem recordings.

Universal insisted that this case did not set a general precedent that labels should pay a licence royalty on digital. Nevertheless, countless other artists sued for higher digital royalties, some securing class action status for their litigation, meaning any artist with a similar contract with the same record company might be able to claim higher royalties if the lawsuits prevailed.

Despite the high number of lawsuits, few cases have reached court and in

25: Though this side of the debate is possibly now underway as songwriters have seen their income drop significantly as digital shifts from downloads to streams.

the main the majors have sought to settle these actions. Though those settlements that have been made public – mainly those relating to class actions – have generally seen the majors offer only slight increases on download royalties, usually with some provision for past royalties and legal costs to date. The outcome is that most artists are seeing at most just a few per cent more for downloads than CD sales, though higher profile legacy artists may have secured more preferential rates via confidential out-of-court arrangements.

It is worth noting that most of these cases focused on download rather than streaming income (relating to a period in time when the former revenue stream vastly outperformed the latter). The argument for a stream being treated as a licence over a sale is surely even stronger than with downloads. Some newer digital royalty lawsuits do cover streams as well, and not all these cases are currently resolved, so this matter could as yet return to court.

RISK AND TRANSPARENCY

Newer record contracts, of course, clearly set out what royalties are due on digital income (possibly also separating out downloads and streams).

Artists may secure a slightly better rate on downloads than CD, and a slightly better rate again on streams over downloads, though they are unlikely to achieve anything close to a 50/50 split on digital, unless working with an independent label that always worked on a 50/50 net revenue share basis (and which would almost certainly be making a significantly lower investment at the outset).

Beyond the above described contractual interpretation disputes, there is a separate debate to be had on what label/artist split is fair on digital. Record companies would argue that they continue to be the primary risk takers in the music industry, and therefore need to keep the majority of the recorded music revenue stream when an investment successfully launches a new artist and/or album.

Though artists and managers, like the songwriters and publishers above, might argue that, while that is true to an extent, surely the risks are less in digital than physical, and therefore labels should be more generous in how they share the profits. And this argument is arguably even stronger for legacy artists where the label recouped on its initial investment long ago, and the costs of getting that catalogue to market are now considerably smaller.

Of course, when it comes to new rather than ambiguous legacy record contracts, the label could argue that if the artist wasn't happy with the splits they are receiving on downloads and streams, they shouldn't have done the deal. And if new talent needs a label's investment – and most do – they may have to accept terms they don't especially like. Though the growth in 'distribution' and 'services' deals arguably offers artists more choice when seeking a label partner, which might ultimately see even new artists secure better royalty rates on streaming. We consider these new deal options further in the 'Deals Guide' in Appendix One.

Of equal if not greater concern to many managers of artists with post-digital record contracts is transparency. To quote many a lawyer, you may be on a 20% split on streaming income, but "20% of what, precisely?"

Under conventional contracts, record companies are allowed to apply discounts and deductions to income before calculating what the artist is due under their revenue share arrangement. Quite what deductions can be made varies from contract to contract, but might include packaging costs, the cost of lost and damaged stock, and fees for international subsidiaries of a record company that provide additional local marketing and distribution services.

These deductions have always been a point of contention between artist and label, especially once the two parties are not actively working together on new content, so that the record company arguably has no real incentive to placate an artist and may instead seek to maximise its own profits by reducing artist royalty payments wherever possible.

If anything, deductions have become more contentious in the digital era, for a number of reasons. Some labels seem to continue making deductions for things that can only apply in the physical age, such as lost or damaged stock. And some

managers question how international subsidiaries can continue to take the same cut of revenue as with physical, when digital distribution and social media activity, for example, could be done on a global basis by the label in the artist's home country.

To be fair, some labels have started to reduce the discounts and deductions made on streaming income, or remove them entirely, especially for new artists. Though in some cases, in particular with heritage acts, a number of discounts and deductions still apply that can greatly reduce the monies the artist receives, as illustrated in the chart across the page.

These problems are exacerbated by the secrecy that surrounds digital deals (more on which below and in the 'Transparency Guide' in Appendix Two) and are further complicated because different labels apply, refer to and report deductions in different ways, making it hard for artists and managers to track what is going on.

FROM THE ROUNDTABLES

Both artists and their representatives felt that the split between labels and artists was outdated. This obviously varies greatly across the industry, because every record deal is different, but the consensus was that labels should be paying artists a higher royalty on streaming than on CDs, and more than just a few per cent higher, again because of a feeling that the labels' risks are lower in digital than in physical.

There was a particularly strong

Deductions and discounts

£1

−30%
for international — 70p

−25%
for packaging — 52.5p

x 15%
royalty to be paid — 7.87p

BUT x 50%
TV advertising campaign — 3.94p

OR/AND x 75%
single release discount — 5.90p/2.95p

OR/AND x 50%
compilation release discount — 3.94p/1.97p

feeling that a higher rate should be paid to heritage artists – who are often still on lower rate legacy deals – in part recognising that digital has greatly reduced the labels' costs in exploiting catalogue.

Some managers hope that the so called 'contract adjustment mechanism' proposed in the European Union as part of its new Copyright Directive, which is currently being considered, might provide a tool to re-open these old record contracts. Though quite how this 'contract adjustment mechanism' – which originates in German law – would work across Europe is unknown. It arguably applies more to session musicians than featured artists.

Both artists and their representatives also raised the issue of discounts and deductions. Some felt that this was actually the bigger issue, and that labels needed to be much more open about exactly what deductions and discounts are being applied to digital income. This would enable an informed debate between labels and managers about what deductions and discounts are appropriate, especially for heritage artists where physical era deductions have sometimes been applied to digital.

MMF'S ACTION POINTS ON DIVISION OF REVENUE

▶ A stream is not a sale or radio and yet is akin to both. Artists and managers accept that song rights should expect a greater share of streaming income that could be somewhere between a sales royalty and a radio compensation. Further

research is needed to provide guidance on one of the fundamental issues of the recorded music industry.

▶ Managers and creators could also investigate and take competition advice on whether the dominance of the three major music companies in both recordings and publishing distorts the market by influencing the retention of the status quo. This power over the relative income flows is to the detriment of creators.

▶ Artists and managers call on record companies to offer better royalty rates to artists on streaming income, especially heritage artists with pre-digital contracts. They will concurrently investigate if applying Performer Equitable Remuneration to streaming might provide a better minimum rate for performers (more on which below).

▶ Managers support the 'contract adjustment mechanism' described in the draft European Copyright Directive, and seek further clarification on how it might work in practical terms. Managers of British artists will also lobby for such a mechanism to be introduced into UK copyright law even if the proposed new Directive comes in to effect after the UK leaves the EU.

▶ The MMF will further explore the label services sector in order to compare and contrast current deals on the market that are available to artists. The 'Deals Guide' in Appendix One is the first part of this work. Ensuring managers are informed on the variations in short term gains and long term debts in different deal types will be a key priority for the MMF. This may result in commercial pressures being put on labels to offer better contract terms.

▶ Managers will continue to call on labels to declare what deductions and discounts are being made on digital income, especially on pre-digital contracts where these are widespread. This information could be used to inform a separate debate within the management community as to which deductions and discounts, if any, are reasonable in the digital age, and then put further moral pressure onto the record companies to address this issue.

▶ Organisations representing songwriters could commission further research into the specific issues facing full-time songwriters in the streaming domain, and assess whether a re-positioning of the split of income between the recording and song rights would go some way to tackling these issues.

7.2 PERFORMER ER AND MAKING AVAILABLE

As mentioned above, although copyright law does not define either downloads or streams, it is generally accepted that the distribution of recorded content through digital channels exploits both the reproduction and performing right elements of the copyright.

But which performing right? Under most systems, the 'performing rights' traditionally cover both the performance and communication controls of the copyright. Which – when it comes to sound recordings – conventionally means, respectively, the playing of recorded music in a public space and the broadcast of recorded music over AM, FM and DAB radio channels or terrestrial, satellite and cable TV networks.

MAKING AVAILABLE RIGHT

Question five: What kind of digital services exploit the conventional performing rights and what kind exploit the specific 'making available right', and should copyright law be more specific on this point?

While it would seem reasonable to suggest that the communication control that covers traditional broadcasting should also cover webcasting – ie radio or TV style services delivered over the internet, and maybe personalised radio too – as mentioned above, in the early days of the world wide web there were concerns about more interactive forms of digital distribution, principally downloads.

To that end a new more specific control called the 'making available right' was formally introduced in World Intellectual Property Organisation treaties in 1996 and in the European Union in 2001, and subsequently added to many individual copyright systems.

According to the WIPO treaty, this applies to electronic transmission "in such a way that members of the public may access the recording from a place and at a time individually chosen by them". So neither broadcasts nor online simulcasts of TV or radio, but definitely downloads and possibly other interactive digital channels too.

Though which interactive digital channels specifically? A distinction has sometimes been made to the effect that personalised radio services should come under the conventional communication control, while fully on-demand streaming platforms should come under the newer making available right.

But not everyone agrees, and there is further confusion in that most fully on-demand streaming services like Spotify also offer a personalised radio option within their platforms.

PERFORMER ER ON DIGITAL

Question six: Should performer equitable remuneration apply to all streaming services, including those exploiting the making available right?

This distinction is not just a semantic one, because of Performer ER. As mentioned above, in most countries Performer ER is due when the performing rights of a sound recording copyright are exploited, but the making available right – despite arguably being a subset of the communication control – is often excluded from this. So if a streaming service is exploiting the conventional communication control Performer ER should be paid, but if the making available right is at play, no automatic (ie non-contractual) payments to performers are due. This makes the ambiguities around the definition of the stream, in terms of copyright law, perplexing for the performer community.

Depending on how making available has been implemented in any one

copyright system, there are two possible arguments against the current approach...

▶ First, that making available should only apply to downloads, meaning that all and any streaming services are exploiting the conventional communication control, meaning Performer ER is due.

▶ Or second, that Performer ER should be due whenever the making available right is exploited anyway, and that the exclusion of Performer ER from making available was a mistake. Depending on how making available was implemented in any one country's copyright system, applying Performer ER to making available may just require a new interpretation of current laws, or – as in the UK – a rewrite of copyright law.

In a small number of European countries it has actually been decided that Performer ER should apply to streams, though it remains to be seen quite how that works out. Meanwhile, as the new European Copyright Directive has gone through the motions in Brussels many artist groups have called for a specific Performer ER right on streaming to be inserted at an EU level, though that measure was not included in the first draft.

If it was decided that Performer ER was due on all streaming income – either by classifying streams as communication rather than making available, or by applying Performer ER to the making available right – digital services would be obliged to pay royalties directly to performers as well as labels, most likely through the collective licensing system. (In the some countries, including the UK, it would be the labels' obligation to ensure performers received ER).

This would mean a significant shift in negotiating power for featured artists unable to secure better digital royalties from their labels, while opening up a new revenue stream for session musicians who usually have no contractual right to a share of digital income, but who would receive ER payments in the same way they do from broadcast and public performance.

What this would mean in real terms – ie what royalties would labels, featured artists and session musicians see if ER was applied to streaming? – would depend on how such a system was applied. Some songwriters and publishers fear that if ER was applied to streams that could result in their share of digital income also being cut, in addition to any cut in the sum received by the labels. That is not the intent of the artist groups lobbying for ER on streams, and would be much less likely in countries like the UK where the ER right is against the rights owner rather than the licensee.

A number of models for applying ER to streams have been proposed. MMF commissioned some research into what each of those models would mean in terms of what each stakeholder would approximately earn. The results of that research are over the page, with an outline of each proposed model in the box on the right. This reserach was based on the

How would ER on streaming work?

The chart on the next page demonstrates the impact different royalty models have on how digital income is shared between labels, featured artists and session musicians. This includes different record deal types with no ER being paid on streaming, and a number of systems where ER is paid on streaming.

These calculations are based on a number of assumptions and are intended as an approximate guide. Assumptions include: Total CMO commissions of 15% (recordings) and 10% (songs); songwriter on a 30/70 split with publisher; and ER where paid is split between featured artists and session musicians 66%/34%.

Artist royalties paid by labels do not account for any discounts or deductions as discussed above. Also, royalties paid by labels to artists may be set off against the record company's unrecouped investment, whereas ER would be paid to the artist whatever.

The different models are as follows:

1. Based on a contractual royalty of 5%.

2. Based on a contractual royalty of 15%.

3. Based on a contractual royalty of 20%.

4. Based on a contractual royalty of 30%.

5. If an ER royalty of 3% was paid direct to artists via CMO, deducted from the label's DSP payment, in addition to a contractual royalty of 20%.

6. If just an ER royalty of 50% was paid on all streaming income direct to artists via CMO.

7. If streaming income was split between reproduction and performing rights 50/50, with reproduction right income shared with artist on a contractual royalty of 20% and a 50/50 ER arrangement applied to performing right income.

8. As 7, but if streaming income was split between reproduction and performing rights 25/75.

9. If just an ER royalty of 30% was paid on all streaming income direct to artists via CMO.

How would ER on streaming work?

| | 5% royalty | 15% royalty | 20% royalty |
	1	2	3
Label	78.9p	70.6p	66.4p
Featured Artist	4.2p	12.5p	16.6p
Session Musician	0.0p	0.0p	0.0p
Recording CMO(s) eg PPL	0.0p	0.0p	0.0p
Publisher	4.6p	4.6p	4.6p
Songwriter	10.7p	10.7p	10.7p
Songs CMO(s) eg PRS	1.7p	1.7p	1.7p

*FOR EVERY ONE POUND PAID TO THE
MUSIC INDUSTRY BY DSPS

30% royalty	3% of total ER	50% of total ER	Reproduction/ Performing Split 1	Reproduction/ Performing Split 2	30% of total ER
4	5	6	7	8	9
58.1p	63.4p	35.3p	50.8p	43.1p	49.4p
24.9p	18.3p	23.3p	19.9p	21.6p	14p
0.0p	0.9p	12p	6p	9p	7.2p
0.0p	0.5p	12.5p	6.2p	9.3p	12.5p
4.6p	4.6p	4.6p	4.6p	4.6p	4.6p
10.7p	10.7p	10.7p	10.7p	10.7p	10.7p
1.7p	1.7p	1.7p	1.7p	1.7p	1.7p

assumption that the introduction of ER on streams would not affect the royalties received by songwriters and publishers.

THE PERFORMER'S MAKING AVAILABLE CONTROL

Question seven: Do record labels need a specific making available waiver from all artists before exploiting their recordings digitally?

There is another area of contention regarding making available. While Performer ER may not apply, making available is, nevertheless, now commonly included in the list of controls provided to recording artists by their performer rights. As with the other performer controls, labels need artists to waive or assign their making available right through contract in order to subsequently exploit that element of the copyright. As such, new artist contracts will specifically state that the performer's making available right is waived or assigned.

But what about legacy contracts which pre-date the addition of the 'making available' right to copyright law in the mid-1990s?

Obviously these contracts cannot include a term specifically waiving the making available control, because there was no such control at the time the contract was written. It could therefore be argued that to exploit the making available right through downloads or streams, a record label must first secure a new agreement with each and every legacy artist waiving this new performer control.

Those artists could then use that moment to negotiate better digital royalties.

However, record companies have generally assumed that all legacy artist contracts already provide them with the right to exploit the making available control. There are two arguments why this might be the case:

▶ Making available is a sub-set of the existing communication control which may be referenced in the original contract.

▶ A vague catch-all term may have been included in the original contract in which the artist waives both current and future performer controls.

However, many artists dispute both these points, arguing that making available is a distinct performer control and that vague catch-all terms are not enforceable. This dispute has been tested in two European lawsuits in recent years. The two key cases to date involved Finnish rock band Hurriganes and Swedish musician Johan Johansson.

In the former case, Hurriganes prevailed in a legal dispute with Universal Music on whether or not a legacy contract could waive a performer control that did not exist at the time the contract was written. Though there was an added complication in this case, in that neither side could actually produce the record contract in question. Johan Johansson, meanwhile, won a lawsuit against the record company MNW over whether it, despite owning the copyright in the recordings on which Johansson appeared, nevertheless had the right to distribute that content to streaming services that exploit the making available right.

These are still relatively recent cases, and appeals may follow, so it remains to be seen if they set a precedent in Finland and Sweden, or beyond. But these cases and/or other future litigation on this issue could as yet confirm that the record companies' assumption regarding making available in relation to legacy contracts is incorrect.

FROM THE ROUNDTABLES

Artists and their representatives felt that Performer ER should perhaps be paid on streaming income, assuring featured artists a guaranteed minimum royalty on streaming revenue. This would also provide a new income stream for session musicians, who are set to lose out if the growth of streaming ultimately results in a decline in the royalties paid by radio stations, on which Performer ER is currently paid.

Label representatives were against Performer ER being paid on streaming income. This was in part because of an assumption that Performer ER would mean a 50/50 split between labels and artists, would require collective licensing of all streaming income, and might equate to compulsory licensing in some countries. Some labels also again argued that their risks remain high and any system that resulted in increased artist royalties could destabilise their business.

Most managers agreed that forcing collective licensing onto the streaming market would be risky, especially if it involved the more effective collecting societies relying on the less effective collecting societies in other markets.

Some also pointed out that the law does not define 'equitable remuneration' and Performer ER need not be a 50/50 split between labels and artists. Plus ER might only be due on the 'performing right' element of the copyright, not the 'reproduction element'. So, if you said a stream was 50% reproduction rights and 50% performing rights, ER would be 50% of 50%, ie 25%. These various possible options were explored in the aforementioned MMF research on the possible financial impact of ER being introduced on streams.

Despite recognising the issues, many managers felt that Performer ER on streaming was still something worth considering, especially if an alternative system could be created for collecting and distributing Performer ER, making it less reliant on collective licensing. This would almost certainly require a change to copyright law though, and what is possible would likely vary from country to country.

MMF'S ACTION POINTS ON PERFORMER ER

▶ Artists and managers will investigate the possible approaches to achieving Performer ER on streaming, and assess if and how that would be possible under different copyright systems.

Elements of the deal

THE MUSIC INDUSTRY'S STREAMING DEALS HAVE MANY ELEMENTS TO THEM

Revenue Share

Minimum Guarantee

Advance?

Fees?

Equity?

▶ The MMF will then consult with other organisations representing artists and managers on whether this is something to campaign for, either by lobbying for a change in or clarification of copyright law, or by pursuing a test case in court on whether a stream constitutes a straight communication or rental, rather than (or in addition to) making available.

▶ Artists and managers will seek confirmation from the labels that they agree Performer ER is definitely due on online radio and personalised radio, and clarification as to how this is paid when such services are licensed directly rather than collectively, especially in the US and UK where the same CMO – ie SoundExchange and PPL respectively – represents both labels and (at least some) performers.

7.3 SHARING THE VALUE OF DIGITAL DEALS

Most of the music industry's deals with the DSPs are confidential, with only a small number of people at each label, publisher or CMO party to the specifics of the arrangement. This means that the non-corporate beneficiaries of the copyrights being exploited by the digital platforms – ie artists and songwriters – are not allowed to know the terms under which those copyrights are being used.

Nevertheless, the basic structure of these arrangements is known, as described above. Most digital deals are ultimately revenue share arrangements, but with the DSP also

committing to minimum guarantees and upfront advances, and possibly additional fees and the provision of equity to the rights owner. Despite not usually knowing the specifics of the deals, many artists and managers have raised concerns about some of these key elements.

EQUITY

Question eight: Should record companies and music publishers demand equity from digital start-ups, and if so should they share the profits of any subsequent share sale with their artists and songwriters, and if so on what terms?

Some rights owners require equity when first licensing start-up streaming businesses. This is particularly true of the three major record companies and the previously referenced indie labels digital rights body Merlin.

As noted above, there is a logic to rights owners taking equity in new DSPs as they license them for the first time. Many of those who invest in new tech start-ups do so assuming they will profit from their investment not when the company itself becomes a profitable concern but when it is sold to an existing major media or tech business, or via an IPO.

It may be that the biggest profits to be made from a start-up business will stem from this first transaction, and if that's when the start-up's backers will profit most, the labels want a cut of that action too.

Most artists and managers understand this logic, but there is still a point of contention: what happens to any profits made if and when the label sells its equity stake in the start-up? The original assumption was that many labels would keep these profits in their entirety, citing clauses in artist contracts that say the record company is only obliged to pay royalties to artists on income directly and identifiably attributable to a specific recording.

Artists and managers argue that this is unfair because the label was only able to demand equity in the first place because of the combined value of its artists' recordings, and therefore artists should share in the profits of any equity sale. Additionally, if labels are not obliged to share this income with artists, they may agree to less favourable terms on revenue share and minimum guarantees, where income is shared with the artists, in return for a better deal on equity.

In one legal battle a few years ago with a group of artists over various royalty disputes, Sony Music unapologetically stated that it was perfectly entitled to structure deals in this way if it so wished. Though many labels would actually counter that the monetary value of any equity stake is uncertain and not accessible for the foreseeable future, so they are unlikely to forego other short-term revenues in return for a better equity deal.

Either way, it should be noted that many labels, including Sony Music, have more recently made commitments to share the profits made when equity secured through licensing deals is sold with their artists. Indeed, many indies made this commitment in 2014 via the World Independent Network's Fair Digital Deals Declaration.

That Declaration included the commitment to: "account to artists a good-faith pro-rata share of any revenues and other compensation from digital services that stem from the monetisation of recordings but are not attributed to specific recordings or performances".

Though, of course, the devil is always in the detail, and exactly how the equity share commitments made by both major and indie record labels will work is still not entirey clear.

ADVANCES

Question nine: Should record companies and music publishers demand large advances from new digital services, and if so should they share any 'breakage' (unallocated advances) with their artists and songwriters, and if so on what terms?

Most rights owners will request upfront advances, often in the millions, from DSPs. A leaked Sony Music deal with Spotify in the US provided a $9 million advance in year one, $16 million in year two, and $17.5 million in an optional third year.

These advances are usually recoupable for the DSP over a set time period, but are non-refundable if revenue share or minimum guarantee-based royalties due in that period do not exceed the advance paid. So if the DSP pays a $1 million advance for the next year, but then the record company's catalogue generates only $750,000 under its revenue share or minimum guarantee arrangement, the rights owner gets to keep the extra $250,000.

Again there is a logic to the advances: many start-ups ultimately deliver little in the way of revenue, initially or ever, so the rights owner wants to build in some guarantees to justify going to the effort of doing the deal. And, in real terms, any business likes to be paid upfront if at all possible. But artists and managers have raised two concerns about the advances.

First, the size of the advances arguably makes it hard for new DSPs to enter the market, because a service needs considerable funds available to pay multi-million advances at the outset. This ultimately reduces consumer choice, and makes it hard for niche services to launch, a concern also expressed by the UK Entertainment Retailers Association in its manifesto document back in 2015.

Second, there is the issue of what happens to unallocated advances, what has often been dubbed as 'breakage'. So in the example above the record company was $250,000 up on the deal, because it was due $750,000 based on the consumption of its repertoire but had been paid a $1 million advance. So what happens to the $250,000? Does the label simply bank the surplus, or does it share it with its artists?

In recent years, all three of the major record companies have made commitments to share any such surplus with artists. Many independents, meanwhile, made a similar commitment via the aforementioned Fair Digital Deals Declaration.

That said, as with the equity share commitment, it remains unclear exactly what these commitments on breakage mean in real terms, ie how surpluses are allocated to artists and when such allocations began.

Some have also noted that once a successful streaming service is established advances are nearly always recouped by the DSP, so there is no surplus. Therefore it may be that some of the major record companies have committed to share these surpluses with artists only now that there isn't any money to share.

OTHER KICKBACKS

Question ten: Should record companies and music publishers demand other kickbacks from new digital services, and if so should they share the benefits with their artists, and if so on what terms?

Rights owners may also receive other kickbacks over and above equity and advances.

The label or publisher may be able to charge administration, technical or legal fees to the DSP, and may receive other benefits, for example in the aforementioned leaked Sony/Spotify contact the record company received an allocation of advertising on the DSP's freemium service which it could use or sell on.

As with equity, many artists and managers fear that rights owners may agree to less favourable terms on key revenue share and minimum guarantee arrangements in return for these extra kickbacks, because the artists must share in the former but can be excluded from the latter. While this may simply be paranoia on the part of artists and managers, the secrecy that surrounds so many digital deals adds to this distrust.

FROM THE ROUNDTABLES

Artists and their representatives felt strongly that labels and publishers should share the profits of all elements of their DSP deals, including the profits that stem from equity, unallocated advances and set-up fees. While opinion was divided on the labels' legal obligations here, it was universally felt that there was an ethical obligation.

Artists and their representatives recognised and welcomed those commitments that had already been made by both major and independent record companies to share any profits stemming from equity sales and unallocated advances.

However, as mentioned above, there remains much confusion as to how these commitments will actually be delivered, with some noting that – especially at the bigger record companies – specifics and sometimes even the basics about these commitments had generally not been communicated internally,

let alone to artists and their representatives. There also remains the unknown as to whether the set-up fees charged by some record companies included a profit margin.

MMF'S ACTION POINTS ON SHARING THE VALUE OF DIGITAL DEALS

▶ Artists and managers call on those labels and publishers yet to fully commit publicly to share the value of equity and/or unallocated advances with their artists to do so, either individually, or by signing up to the Worldwide Independent Network's Fair Deals Declaration.

▶ Artists and managers call upon labels and publishers to explain in more detail to all contracted artists how previous commitments to share the value of digital deals will be delivered, and to be more specific about which equity and unallocated advances the commitments relate to. In addition the MMF will seek explanations as to what the upfront fees relate to and whether any profit is made on those fees.

7.4 TRANSPARENCY

Question eleven: Can it be right that the beneficiaries of copyright are not allowed to know how their songs and recordings are being monetised, and should a new performer right ensure that information is made available to artists, songwriters and their representatives?

The lack of clarity over the value of each different aspect the labels' digital deals brings us to the issue most commonly raised by artists and managers regarding the streaming business, the secrecy that surrounds each arrangement, which means that artists and songwriters, despite being beneficiaries of music copyrights, are not allowed to know how these copyrights are being valued or exploited. When managers seek clarity on these issues, they are often told that non-disclosure agreements, or NDAs, in the contracts between the labels and the DSPs mean information cannot be shared.

While there is a tendency for both rights owners and DSPs to blame each other for the 'NDA culture' that has grown up around the digital music market, it seems likely that the wide ranging non-disclosure agreements that surround most digital deals were originally requested by the services, they being so common in the tech sector. Though it seems that many rights owners have overly embraced the NDAs in subsequent years, usually citing competition concerns for the need for secrecy.

Of course, any company wants a degree of confidentiality around its commercial deals, so confidentiality clauses are common in any contractual agreements. And rights owners might argue that their negotiating hands would be weakened if each new digital service knew precisely what deal its competitors had secured, and a weaker negotiating hand would be to the detriment of all the stakeholders in music copyright.

However, as a result of the secrecy surrounding the music industry's digital deals, artists and songwriters, despite being beneficiaries of music copyright, are in the dark as to how those copyrights are being commercialised. This results in a number of problems:

▶ It makes it hard for artists and songwriters to properly audit the royalties they receive to ensure they are being paid what they are contractually due.

▶ It makes it hard for artists and songwriters to assess whether, in their opinion, a label, publisher or CMO is behaving in a fair way, an assessment that could affect the artist or songwriter's subsequent deals and agreements.

▶ It makes it hard for artists and songwriters to assess whether a label, publisher or CMO is securing the best deals and processing payments in the most efficient way, an assessment that could affect the artist or songwriter's subsequent deals and agreements.

▶ It makes it hard for artists and songwriters to assess the relative value of their music being consumed on rival digital platforms.

▶ These facts inevitably result in a breakdown of trust between labels and artists, and publishers and songwriters, and/or public criticism of digital services by high profile artists and songwriters which may or may not be justified.

Beyond these many and various issues, it could be argued that there is an ethical element to this debate.

Can it be right that a legal beneficiary of a copyright can be deprived of crucial information required to calculate exactly what benefit they are due? Should the right to such information be a moral right under contract or copyright law? And should the right to information about the exploitation of a sound recording be added as a new additional performer right?

A report published by Berklee College Of Music's Rethink Music programme in 2015 proposed a Creators Bill Of Rights, which includes the line "every creator deserves to know the entire payment stream for his/her royalties (eg which parties are taking a cut and how much)". Meanwhile in France, a government-led initiative involving artists and labels resulted in a code of conduct under which the latter, in the words of the International Federation Of The Phonographic Industry, would seek to "bring greater clarity and understanding on the distribution of revenues to different parties".

In Europe, transparency is one of the issues addressed in the aforementioned draft Copyright Directive.

Article 14 of that draft states that: "Member States shall ensure that authors and performers receive on a regular basis and taking into account the specificities of each sector, timely, adequate and sufficient information on the exploitation of their works and performances from those to whom they have licensed or transferred their rights, notably as regards modes

of exploitation, revenues generated and remuneration due".

Managers are hopeful that, in Europe, that article of the directive might help address ongoing transparency issues, though it remains to be seen how the final draft is worded, and how that measure is implemented.

FROM THE ROUNDTABLES

At the roundtables, many managers identifed transparency as one of the single biggest issues in relation to the streaming business.

Those discussions confirmed the viewpoint expressed in our earlier survey of artist managers: that — while NDAs may be necessary — artists, songwriters and managers should be brought 'inside the NDA', so that they too know the specifics of the digital deals.

Of course there are a lot of artists, songwriters and managers, and it could be argued that once you have hundreds if not thousands of people 'inside the NDA', the confidentiality clause becomes unenforceable, because the information will inevitably leak and it would be impossible to identify who did the leaking.

A possible compromise is that artists and songwriters are allowed to request that their accountants have access to this information for auditing purposes, which would overcome some though not all of the problems outlined above. This would reduce the number of people party to the confidential information, and given accountants are usually subject to specific professional standards, it would provide some formality as to how the information is used.

Some managers suggested there may be other reasons for the lack of transparency in addition to the NDAs. That might include a need-to-know culture at the labels, publishers and CMOs; a lack of resource to communicate complex and ever-evolving deals; and ignorance at the top of some music companies that this information is even required. Many managers also felt that some labels and publishers may be benefiting from the lack of transparency financially.

On the other side, managers conceded that they probably needed to be more specific when demanding more transparency. Most labels, publishers and CMOs agree more transparency is required, and most argue they are being more transparent already. Which is probably true to an extent. But what specific data and information do artists and managers need?

MMF'S ACTION POINTS ON TRANSPARENCY

▶ Artists and managers will agree what information is required, publish it and clearly state this to all labels and publishers. This information has now been published in the 'Transparency Guide' that is included in Appendix Two.

▶ Artist and managers support Article 14 of the proposed European Copyright Directive and its proposal to introduce a 'transparency obligation' incumbent upon rights owners. They will also seek more clarity on what that transparency obligation would cover and will promote the above mentioned list of what information is required by artists and managers to law-makers as well as labels and publishers. Clarity should also be sought on the proposed limitations of the 'transparency obligation', so as to ensure it will be enforceable in practical terms.

▶ Managers of British artists will also lobby for such an obligation to be introduced into UK copyright law even if the proposed new Directive comes in to effect after the UK leaves the European Union.

▶ Artists and managers will ask DSPs to publicly state that they would be happy for key deal information to be shared with artists and their representatives as some have already said this off-the-record.

▶ Managers will seek assurances from competition regulators in key countries that the sharing of key deal information with artists and their representatives would not result in action being taken on competition law grounds.

▶ Artists and managers will push for royalty as well as consumption data to be shared directly with artists and their representatives by the DSPs, so that managers can better audit digital royalties and what happens to income as it passes through a label or publisher.

▶ Managers could champion the most transparent labels and publishers

ISSUES & VIEWPOINTS

103

which adopt best practice in sharing deal information and digital royalty reporting. The 'Transparency Index' outlined in the 'Transparency Guide' will help with this process.

7.5 SAFE HARBOURS AND OPT-OUT SERVICES

Question twelve: Should the safe harbours in European and American law be revised so companies like YouTube and SoundCloud cannot benefit from them, however good their takedown systems may or may not be?

Both American and European law provides protection for internet companies which provide tools or channels used by others to distribute copyright works without licence. These protections originate in America's Digital Millennium Copyright Act 1998 and the European Union's Electronic Commerce Directive 2000/31 and are commonly referred to within the industry as 'safe harbours'.

HOW THE SAFE HARBOURS WORK

From a copyright perspective, the safe harbours were intended to protect the then emerging market occupied by internet service providers, server hosting companies and similar businesses from financial and criminal liability for copyright infringement if and when those companies' customers used the internet access or web storage they bought to distribute copyright infringing material.

Early on, internet companies argued that without such protection from liability, their business models would become unfeasible – owing to the difficulty of identifying infringing content amongst incredibly high volumes of traffic – and that growth in internet usage would therefore be curtailed

A condition of the safe harbour protection is that the internet company has a system in place via which copyright owners can flag copyright infringing content or material, and that the internet firm then removes this content once made aware of it. These are often called 'takedown systems', and people in the music industry often refer to 'DMCA takedowns', even in Europe where it is European law rather than the DMCA that actually applies.

The quality of the takedown systems operated by websites claiming safe harbour protection vary greatly. Nevertheless, rights owners now routinely issue large numbers of takedown notices to such companies, with the US and UK record industry being particularly prolific in this domain.

THE DEBATE OVER WHAT KINDS OF SERVICES SHOULD HAVE PROTECTION

Over the last few years representatives of the record industry and music publishing sector have begun to argue that these safe harbours are being used by a much more diverse range of businesses than was originally intended by lawmakers in Europe and the US.

The kind of business the labels and publishers are mainly thinking about here are user-upload platforms like YouTube and SoundCloud, where users upload audio or video files to the DSP's servers – some of it including other people's copyright work without the requisite licenses having been obtained – and then the DSP aggregates that content.

This content is then accessible from a central home page and search engine, and users can organise it into playlists. The outcome of this process is that sites like YouTube and SoundCloud soon boast music libraries very similar (and often larger) to those of services like Spotify, and therefore start to compete with those platforms.

But unlike Spotify, which accesses content as a result of its licensing deals with the record companies, the user-upload services do not rely solely on the labels to provide the music. Instead, any labels and publishers that do not wish their content to appear on these platforms must issue takedown notices (and/or pursue legal action against the actual individual uploaders, which is not a desirable option).

From the rights owners' perspective, this makes these 'opt-out' rather than 'opt-in' streaming services. Some labels and publishers believe this runs contrary to the basic principle of copyright: ie the rights of the copyright owner extend beyond the mere right to have content removed in hindsight, and that permission should always be sought before a copyright work is exploited, even if that is a tricky process.

That said, these rights owners are not objecting to the concept of safe harbours outright, recognising the practicalities that led to their introduction in the first place. Rather, they are questioning whether user-upload platforms – which are arguably content providers as well as providers of internet services – should enjoy protection. This poses a number of questions...

▶ Does US and European law as it is currently written provide user-upload platforms with safe harbour protection? The operators of such platforms would almost certainly answer with an unequivocal "yes", arguing that legal precedent is on their side. Rights owners might argue that current law is less clear cut than that and still open to interpretation.

▶ Even if current law does provide these services with safe harbour protection, should it? Did lawmakers in the 1990s ever imagine services like YouTube and SoundCloud benefiting from the safe harbours? And even if they did, is the current situation having a sufficiently detrimental affect on copyright and/or the copyright industries to justify a rethink?

Of course some user-upload services – including both YouTube and SoundCloud – have actually sought licenses from the music industry. These licenses allow rights owners to upload and monetise content on these platforms themselves, and also to claim and monetise (or remove) any songs or recordings they own which have been uploaded to the platform by third parties.

Most notable in this domain is YouTube, which has long-established licensing deals with many, and probably most, music rights owners, and which has built a system called Content ID to help rights owners monitor, remove and monetise content uploaded by third parties (whether that content is audio-only, an official music video, a cover version of a published song, or a recording synced to a third party video).

Nevertheless, many rights owners who have benefited from these licensing deals remain critical. The argument goes that the safe harbours give YouTube an unfair advantage in licensing negotiations, because it can basically say "we have your content already, either license us on our terms, or you'll be left with the cost of monitoring our networks on a daily basis". User-upload services might counter that rights owners always have to dedicate some resource to monitoring unlicensed use of their content, while YouTube could argue that Content ID removes many of the costs anyway.

Though rights owners would likely say that no automated rights management system is 100% reliable and there will always be admin costs associated with running even a Content ID account; all of which makes it harder for rights owners to walk away from the negotiating table.

This, some labels and publishers argue, results in licensed user-upload services getting preferential rates creating a 'value gap' in the music rights sector.

THE DEBATE OVER TAKEDOWN SYSTEMS

There is a second element to the debate around safe harbours in the music industry: how sophisticated should the takedown systems be? Many music rights owners now issue takedown notices on an industrial scale against sites that claim safe harbour protection. But as recordings are removed from said sites, exact replacements are often immediately uploaded by users to the same platforms. Rights owners are therefore required to constantly monitor these sites for new uploads and to issue a flood of new takedown notices each day. This process has commonly been compared to a game of Whac-A-Mole.

The music industry would prefer more sophisticated takedown systems so that when a recording is removed from any one site for the first time it then stays down, ie the site takes measures to ensure it is not re-uploaded. But how sophisticated a takedown system must websites operate in order to enjoy safe harbour protection? There is some ambiguity here, though the American courts have not generally set the bar particularly high with regards what a takedown system should look like under the DMCA.

Rights owners suspect some user-upload platforms operate deliberately poor takedown systems because their business models rely on a steady stream of copyright infringing content.

For example, some in the music industry criticised the takedown system operated by the now defunct user-upload streaming service Grooveshark. Though the litigation that led to that service's closure centred on music allegedly uploaded by staff rather than users, so didn't test safe harbour law.

The long-running criminal action against the defunct file-transfer service MegaUpload, if it ever reaches court, may further consider what American law says about takedowns; or specifically, whether safe harbours should still apply if a company can be shown to have been 'willfully blind' about users distributing content without licence and/or to have encouraged such activity, even if a nominal takedown system was in place.

Of course in Content ID, YouTube has built what is probably the most sophisticated takedown system. Though, as noted, that doesn't mean it is 100% reliable, and to date it has been much more effective for managing recording rather than song rights on the video platform. That said, YouTube continues to evolve the technology, and the music community might benefit from being more vocal and more clear on what it would like this system – and any other takedown system for that matter – to achieve.

WHERE DO USER-UPLOAD PLATFORMS FIT IN?

As work began in Brussels on preparing a new copyright directive, the music rights industry put safe harbours at the top of its lobbying agenda. Article 13 of the draft directive seeks to address the music industry's concerns.

The music industry argues that, however the law may have been interpreted over the years, safe harbours were never intended for user-upload services like YouTube, and that said services have in effect been exploiting a loophole in the law to build massive content platforms without paying market-rate royalties (or any, in some cases) to copyright owners.

The music industry is basically asking for lawmakers to revise the safe harbour to exclude services like YouTube – which build a consumer-facing streaming service out of their user's uploaded content – from safe harbour protection.

On one level this is an issue that unites the wider music industry, in that trade groups representing labels, publishers, collective management organisations, artists and songwriters have all called for safe harbour rules to be revisited in this way.

That said, there are some side debates. YouTube often implies that without the safe harbours it could not operate as a viable business, because it would have to manually monitor every single upload to its platform, which would be far too cost prohibitive. And the last thing marketing teams at record companies want is to kill off YouTube, it being one of the most important marketing channels in the modern music business.

There is also an argument that, with Content ID, YouTube has actually helped the music industry create new revenue streams, monetising previously lost or forgotten content that users rather than rights owners have digitised, and creating new income from user-generated content and bedroom-produced cover versions.

And, with consumers sharing unlicensed content in numerous ways online, it could be argued that there are benefits for rights owners in having this sharing occur on platforms where rights can be more effectively managed and monetised.

If a change to safe harbour rules really did result in a cut-back YouTube, these benefits of Content ID could go too. Though more bullish music industry executives might argue that YouTube's claim it could not operate without safe harbour protection is a bluff, and therefore there is less to lose than it might seem.

Yes, YouTube might have to invest in order to more proactively monitor uploads to its networks, but given the revenues the service presumably generates, coupled with the valuable data and traffic it provides for the wider Google network, some think that that is an investment the company would make, if it had to. Not

least because the removal of safe harbours for its direct competitors would give YouTube a competitive advantage, in that it is better positioned to take on monitoring duties than its rivals.

But nevertheless, YouTube and many other tech firms are opposing safe harbour reform in Europe. They cite concerns about the wider impact such changes might have on other online businesses, such as social networks where users routinely post photos and articles owned by third parties without permission.

As we said, a key reason why rights owners are now lobbying on the safe harbour issue is the perceived 'value gap' that they argue the existence of user-upload platforms has created in the digital music market. Most user-upload platforms are free-to-access and, where monetisation is possible, are usually ad-funded. But many in the music community are frustrated that ad-funded platforms enjoy much bigger audiences to paid-for services, but generate much less income.

Though it seems inevitable that the digital music market will always be based around a majority who consume via low-value (for the industry) platforms and a minority who use high-value premium services.

The challenge is growing ad revenues to increase the value of the free services, and to find better ways to convert freemium users into premium users, either by the user-upload services upselling their own pay-to-use packages, or having them

The data we need

- [ ] What is the ISRC of the recording?

- [ ] What song is this a recording of?

- [ ] What is the ISWC of that song?

- [ ] Who is the featured artist?

- [ ] What other performers appear on the recording?

- [ ] Who wrote the song?

- [ ] Who owns the copyright in the recording in this country?

- [ ] Who owns the copyright in the song in this country?

- [ ] If there are multiple owners, what are the splits?

- [ ] Which CMO or CMOs represent the copyright owners in the recording?

- [ ] Which CMO or CMOs represent the performer's ER rights?

- [ ] Which CMO or CMOs represent the songwriters?

- [ ] Are the mechanical rights in this song controlled by the publisher or the CMO?

integrate better with other premium platforms.

The music industry knows it must now rise to this challenge, and would likely say that lobbying for safe harbour reform is part of that process. Though it should continue to concurrently explore ways that both ad revenue and premium upsell on the user-upload platforms can be increased.

FROM THE ROUNDTABLES

Most roundtable participants shared the concerns about safe harbours and the way opt-out streaming services are licensed, but some managers were pessimistic about the industry achieving tangible reform. Though we should note that the draft Copyright Directive was published after those debates.

At the roundtables, some managers also pointed out the benefits YouTube in particular delivers as a marketing channel and micro-licensing platform. Some managers also stressed that transparency issues made it hard for them to truly assess the merits, or not, of YouTube compared to services like Spotify and Apple Music.

MMF'S ACTION POINTS ON SAFE HARBOUR

▶ Artists and managers will continue to support the wider music industry's campaign on safe harbours – including further lobbying efforts around Article 13 of the proposed European Copyright Directive – and also continue to stress that a deal on transparency throughout the

value chain is essential in reaching an agreement for the whole music industry.

▶ Beyond safe harbour reform, managers may also want to take the lead and consider possible 'Plan B' initiatives to tackle the wider challenges around opt-out streaming services, including wider discussions on how content is monetised and value is shared, and possible PR and technology solutions that could drive consumers to those services that offer the best deal for the music community, and/or pressure opt-out streaming services to agree to a better deal.

7.6 COPYRIGHT DATA

Question thirteen: How is the music rights industry rising to the challenge of processing usage data and royalty payments from streaming services, what data demands should artists and songwriters be making of their labels, publishers and CMOs, and is a central database of copyright ownership ultimately required?

As mentioned above, the shift from downloads to streams has created significant data challenges for the music industry. Whereas before rights owners needed to know each time a single track or album was sold in order to calculate what they were due from a retailer or download store, now they need to know every single time every single track is listened to by every single user. This has resulted in a flood of usage data for labels, publishers and CMOs to process.

At the same time, whereas each line of 'sales' data would relate to at least pennies of income and often (for the label at least) pounds, each 'listen' will generate fractions of a penny in revenue. Data processing and any subsequent auditing, therefore, must be as efficient as possible, so that administration costs do not eat up all the revenue.

There are, of course, technology solutions to this problem, and rights owners have started to invest in building or buying in such systems. But this has been a steep learning curve and it's highly likely that data processing and therefore revenue distribution was not perfect when the streaming services first started to gain momentum.

Indeed the music rights sector is still tackling this challenge, and for labels, publishers and CMOs, developing such systems is an often hidden cost, with many on the outside seeing streaming as a much cheaper model for the rights owners, which it ultimately might be, but in the short term shifting to this new model has required considerable investment. Nevertheless, artists and songwriters should continue to put pressure on their business partners in this domain, not least by considering data processing abilities when deciding which labels, partners and CMOs to work with.

The data problem is exacerbated by the lack of a central database of copyright ownership information, which limits what the DSPs can do to help with this process. This is more of a problem for songwriters and publishers.

As outlined above, the DSP assumes that whichever label or distributor provides it with a track controls the recording copyright, and therefore should receive usage data and royalties linked to that recording. However, the label or distributor does not tell the DSP who controls the song copyright, and there is no central database where it can access that information.

As we said, this means the DSP has to provide every publisher and every CMO it has a relationship with a complete list of all content usage every month so each rights owner can work out what it is due. This significantly increases the data each and every rights owner has to process, as well as delaying payments whenever there is a dispute between two rights owners about who should be paid for the use of a specific work (ie two publishers between them claim to own 120% of a specific song).

Attempts by the music publishing sector to build a publicly accessible Global Repertoire Database, with an inbuilt system to settle disputes where multiple rights owners claim ownership of the same work, collapsed in 2014. Though the introduction of the copyright hubs in Europe – and another initiatives – mean more CMOs are now sharing data to create regional repertoire databases. And, as mentioned above, some hope that, if similar collaborations take place around the world, these RRDs could eventually be merged to create something like the GRD.

However, to be truly effective, these data projects need to bring together key information about both recordings and songs. Which some do, but not all.

The resulting databases also need to be publicly accessible, at least in part. Again, some initiatives – both industry driven and otherwise – are making some data public, or intend to. Though there is still much work to be done in this domain.

FROM THE ROUNDTABLES

Pretty much everyone agreed that bad music rights data is making the processing of digital royalties inefficient, though there was less consensus on what the solution may be.

Many managers feel that the CMOs are best equipped to tackle this challenge, and should therefore be encouraged to do so. In particular, record industry and publishing sector CMOs should be encouraged to collaborate to identify which songs appear in which recordings.

But not everyone agrees that the CMOs should lead on this, some questioning whether rivalries between societies, or a fear that better data could further reduce the role of the collecting societies in digital licensing, will hinder their efforts. There are a number of private businesses – many start-ups – also working on solutions.

MMF'S ACTION POINTS ON COPYRIGHT DATA

▶ Artists and managers should debate whether to support specific data initiatives or embrace all credible projects.

▶ Managers should encourage all data projects to enable artists, songwriters and their representatives to easily input information about new works into any databases created where that is the best approach.

▶ Managers should ensure that they are aware of what data is required to enable efficient payment of digital royalties, and where to check and amend this data. Organisations like the MMF will provide guidance and training in this area.

7.7 COLLECTIVE LICENSING

Question fourteen: Are streaming services best licensed direct or through collective management organisations; if direct what is the best solution when societies actually control elements of the copyright; and are artists and songwriters actually told what solutions have been adopted?

As we have mentioned above, sometimes digital services are licensed through the music industry's collective licensing system, and sometimes through direct deals with rights owners.

In the main, beyond webcasts that are basically online versions of radio, and those covered by the SoundExchange compulsory licence in the US, the record industry has chosen to license most digital services directly.

Whereas publishers more often license digital collectively, sometimes because the CMOs themselves control key elements of the copyright so can't be cut out of the licensing equation, and sometimes because the CMOs have the best song ownership data so are best positioned to calculate and distribute royalties. Though, as we have seen, the big publishers are now licensing Anglo-American repertoire direct in many cases, especially in Europe, albeit in partnership with the CMOs.

Given collective licensing was traditionally used where you had licensees using large amounts of music but paying relatively low royalties per-usage, you could argue that it would make more sense for all streaming services to be licensed in this way.

And many artists and songwriters would prefer this approach, possibly because they trust their CMO more than their label or publisher; or because payments via CMOs often circumvent contractual terms that enable labels or publishers to retain income; or because they feel collective licensing is fairer to all, because everyone earns the same per play fees, rather than bigger artists or rights owners having a better deal.

That said, the labels and bigger publishers would argue that there are many benefits to direct deals.

Collective licensing regulations in law, and each CMO's own rules, can slow down deal making and reduce the strength of the rights owner's negotiating hand. CMOs are not always empowered or equipped to negotiate the multi-territory licences digital services need. And not all CMOs are so transparent about how money is processed, resulting in ambiguities and delays.

So there are pros and cons to involving the CMOs. Though where the involvement of CMOs is either attractive or – as with publishing in Europe – necessary, because of the rights the societies control, it is possible that a widespread review of both the statutory regulation of collective licensing and each CMO's own rules and regulations is required. Certainly some of the issues raised by songwriters and publishers in relation to digital licensing are as much to do with their own CMO's rules as they are the way the DSPs are doing business.

It maybe that the collective licensing of digital actually needs to be separated from other forms of collective licensing, with the former operating on a global basis, while the latter continues to operate on a territory by territory basis.

You sense this is the message being implied by AMRA, the collecting society bought and relaunched by Kobalt, which seeks to represent the digital rights of publishers and songwriters on a global basis. Some other CMOs also seem to have global ambitions in the digital space.

FROM THE ROUNDTABLES

The roundtables confirmed that artists and songwriters generally prefer collective licensing, and would like more digital services licensed this way, for the various reasons outlined above.

Managers recognise that, while their artists and songwriters may prefer collective licensing, there can be problems with the CMO model.

While there are good collecting societies, there are also less efficient CMOs, and the latter may be relied upon to collect some international royalties.

Some CMOs are slow decision makers, lack transparency and charge high commissions and fees. In some countries courts or statutory bodies can intervene, which can result in royalties being driven down.

MMF'S ACTION POINTS ON COLLECTIVE LICENSING

▶ Artists and managers will put pressure on the CMOs to address the specific issues with collective licensing and highlight those who are following best practice. This includes applying many of the transparency recommendations above to the collecting societies too.

▶ In Europe, artist and managers could communicate the issues – especially around transparency – to whichever government agency has been given an oversight role by the CRM Directive. In the UK this would be the Intellectual Property Office.

▶ Managers will consider which of the other issues raised in this report could be better addressed through a collective rather than direct licensing approach.

▶ Artists and managers call on labels, publishers and CMOs to be much more clear on which services are being licensed directly and with what rights and which ones are licensed collectively in which territories.

7.8 ADAPTING TO THE NEW BUSINESS MODELS

Question fifteen: Is the biggest challenge for the music industry simply adapting to a new business model which pays out based on consumption rather than sales, and over a much longer time period; and what can artists and songwriters do to better adapt?

One final challenge for the wider music community is simply adapting to a new business model, where rather than a record company setting a wholesale price for each record sold, income from which is then shared between label, publisher, artist and songwriter, instead the music industry receives a monthly cut of monies generated by streaming platforms, which is then divided up between stakeholders based on consumption.

This new model means that repeat listening rather than first week sales is key, and monies will come in over a much longer period of time, rather than via a quick spike after an album is launched.

It also means that records and songs that fans listen to again and again over a long period of time will be more lucrative, whereas previously albums that consumers stopped listening to soon after purchase made just as much money for the music industry as albums that were played on a regular basis for years.

And whereas songwriters who contributed to 'filler' songs that consumers perhaps used to skip would still earn their cut under the CD model, they will not under the steaming system, where only those tracks on an album that are actually played earn royalties.

Much of this is stating the obvious of course. Except that critics of the streaming music model often apply old metrics to the new business.

As we said at the outset, it's not a given that the streaming service licensing models that have been developed over the last ten years are the best, the fairest or the most efficient way of doing business.

Though, however these models evolve in the future, labels, publishers, artists and songwriters will have to adapt to the fact their music will generate income in different ways and on different timescales.

Some verbatim quotes from the Digital Dollar roundtables

ON DIVISION OF REVENUE

66 It's sometimes said there is no money in streaming, but that's simply not true. Music makes good money from streaming. There is good revenue coming in. The issue is how that money gets shared 99

66 OK, we are not manufacturing and we are not putting CDs on a truck. But those two elements were actually a tiny bit of the cost of putting out music anyway,

probably less than 10%. The biggest costs when putting out music are A&R, marketing and the label's overheads. Those haven't changed 99

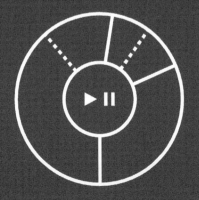

66 Should the labels still be getting the largest slice of the pie, when they have no manufacturing costs, no distribution costs? You could argue the marketing costs have gone up, but it seems to me all the other costs on the record company's side have essentially come down 99

66 For professional songwriters whose only income is on the publishing side – as it is set up now, it's appalling. Their income is diminishing drastically – I know, because I see the royalty statements – that side of the business is being decimated 99

ON PERFORMER ER

66 It seems obvious to me that there should be equitable remuneration on streaming income 99

66 If we had ER on streams, it would need to be a minimum rate, because artist deals vary so much. Artists with distribution deals may be getting a higher rate already than what we are proposing they would get from equitable remuneration 99

66 It seems wrong to me that session musicians receive nothing from streams. If radio income does peak, that's going to be a big issue for many session musicians 99

ON SHARING THE VALUE OF DIGITAL DEALS

66 There have been commitments on sharing the value which is great, but we need a lot more clarity. For example, with one of my artists, I look for the breakage payments on the royalty statements and they're not there. So I go back to the label, and people there don't seem sure. Then they confirm it should be paid 99

66 Everyone thinks of our Spotify equity as a massive windfall, but if we take Spotify's current valuation, it's about

66 Because of the total lack of transparency, you often don't know the question you need to ask – and that's the big problem. If you don't know what's going on you can't properly assess how the label arrived at x, y or z 99

66 It's not necessarily that there shouldn't be NDAs, but artist representatives should be brought into them 99

the equivalent of one month of digital royalties – which is nice to have, and we will share it with our artists – but it's not quite the treasure chest many people assume 99

ON SAFE HARBOUR

ON TRANSPARENCY

66 The single biggest issue is the total lack of transparency. How can we all work together to grow the streaming market when we are not allowed to know which services most benefit our artists? 99

66 We know many fans use YouTube as it if was a streaming platform like Spotify – they minimise the browser and use it as an audio service – but we earn so much less, that's the problem 99

66 YouTube is such a great marketing channel ... such a great discovery platform ... it's difficult to see how new artists could work without it 99

❝ For me, the issues of safe harbours and transparency are closely aligned. Obviously we all want the paid-for services to grow – and we all want the best royalties we can get – and perhaps certain services exploiting the safe harbour are distorting the market. But when all the deals are shrouded in so much secrecy, it's hard for me to have an informed opinion on these issues and where our priorities should lie **❞**

ON COPYRIGHT DATA

❝ As an industry, we have to rise to the challenge on music rights data. It's crazy to blame the streaming services for our poor data **❞**

❝ Certain collecting societies are already working on the data challenge and are making great progress. I really think that's where the solution is going to come from **❞**

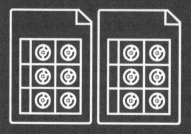

ON COLLECTIVE LICENSING

❝ It just seems more logical – and fair – to me if everyone gets paid the same per stream; so how much you earn is based on how often you get played. And that's what collective licensing allows **❞**

❝ I believe in collective licensing, I prefer it. But if you were starting over – and didn't have any legacy infrastructure in music publishing – I don't think you'd use the collecting societies to license digital. They'd possibly still process the data, but not be the deal makers **❞**

❝ The CMOs are membership organisations, yet members aren't allowed to know the fundamentals of the streaming deals. This seems bizarre to me **❞**

APPENDIX ONE:
THE DEALS GUIDE

WELCOME TO THE DEALS GUIDE

One of the outcomes of the 'Dissecting The Digital Dollar' roundtable debates was the consensus that artists and managers needed to be better informed about the various different kinds of label and distribution deals that are now available in the streaming age, and to have a fuller understanding of the pros and cons of each different approach.

That way managers will be better able to advise their artists on what deals best suit their objectives. And, by having more options on the table, managers should be able to achieve better terms with key partners.

This Deals Guide seeks to do just that by identifying, assessing and explaining ten key deal types.

Introduction

The music business is made up of companies and individuals who work with artists to help them unlock revenue around their music, their performance and their fanbase. Most music companies specialise in a specific revenue stream, meaning an artist will have multiple business partners at any one time.

A key job of the artist manager – as the one business partner involved in all aspects of an artist's career – is to help their clients identify and select the other business partners and to then negotiate specific deals with each of them. And to then manage the relationship between the artist and each business partner on a day-to-day basis.

The record company – or record label – is the business partner that works with the artist on creating and exploiting their recorded music. The label has always been seen as a key business partner for the artist – especially with new talent – because

as well as helping artists create and distribute recordings, they also provide investment and marketing which can help the artist build their fanbase and therefore their wider business.

Over the last ten years the artist/label relationship has started to evolve, partly as a result of changes in the economics of recorded music, partly as a result of the emergence of digital distribution and marketing channels, and partly as a result of the expanded role of the artist manager.

Record labels – or companies that provide the services of a record label (which may call themselves labels, distributors or label services companies) – remain key business partners, especially for new talent, but the nature of the partnership has changed. This guide looks at the different ways artists and labels work together, the kinds of deals available to artists today, and the pros and cons of different artist/label models.

One: The Services A Label Partner Might Provide

Although primarily focused on the artist's recorded music, and the revenues associated with those recordings, labels may provide a wide range of services to the artists they work with. These might include all or any of the following:

ADVANCE
Upfront cash provided to the artist. For new talent, this cash injection may allow an artist to focus on their music full time for the first time. The hope is that, by going full time, an artist can focus on growing their

fanbase and, in turn, boost each of their respective revenue streams. The label isn't necessarily the only business partner to advance cash, though a label advance would traditionally be the most significant.

RECORDING COSTS
The label often organises and pays for the recording of the artist's music. This would involve covering the costs associated with hiring studio space, record producers, sound and mastering engineers, and any session musicians. Under UK copyright law, by organising and paying for the recordings to be made, the label would be the default owner of the sound recording copyright in those tracks.

ARTIST DEVELOPMENT
The label may support the artist's creative development. This may be simply through informal feedback, or by funding songwriting and recording sessions, or by organising collaborations with other artists, songwriters and record producers.

PRODUCT DEVELOPMENT
Once recording sessions are complete, various recorded music products will be created including single, album and EP releases. The label will usually work in liaison with artist and management to decide what form these products will take, and then commission and pay for accompanying visuals such as photography, artwork and videos.

DIGITIAL DISTRIBUTION
The label arranges for completed tracks to be made available to all relevant download stores and streaming platforms. Some labels have their own infrastructure to deliver this content and deals in place with the digital services, while others will utilise the infrastructure and/or deals of third parties.

PHYSICAL MANUFACTURE & DISTRIBUTION
If physical products are to be released – ie CD or vinyl – the label will arrange for these products to be both manufactured and delivered to high street and mail-order retailers. Again, labels may have their own physical distribution network or may utilise the infrastructure of third parties. Several logistics partners may be involved to get product from the factory to the high street.

CONSUMER MARKETING
As a recording is first released a consumer-facing marketing campaign will be staged to promote both the artist and the record. Labels normally lead on this marketing activity, putting together a campaign plan in liaison with artist and management, and then delivering the campaign, either in house or by employing third party agencies.

Traditionally most marketing campaigns would be structured around an album release, with about twelve weeks of activity leading up to and after the release date. Though with the shift to streaming - where repeat listening rather than first week sales are the objective - longer campaigns are often necessary.

An album marketing campaign will

WHAT DOES YOUR PARTNER PROVIDE?

- [ ] Cash Advance
- [ ] Recording Costs
- [ ] Artist Development
- [ ] Product Development
- [x] Digital Distribution
- [ ] Physical Manufacture
- [ ] Physical Distribution
- [ ] Consumer Marketing
- [ ] B2B Marketing
- [ ] Press
- [ ] Promotions
- [ ] Social & Digital
- [ ] Sync

likely include press and promotions work, social media and email activity, and possibly advertising, events and publicity stunts. For the label, the priority is generating sales and/or streams of the record, though for the artist – especially with new talent – the album campaign is as much about building their brand and fanbase, so to grow their other revenue streams as well.

B2B MARKETING

In addition to the consumer-facing marketing campaign, the label will also promote the artist and their recordings to an industry audience. This traditionally meant sales activity to persuade retailers to stock the record. In the digital domain, the digital service provider allows any recordings to be pushed into its platform, so the B2B marketing is more about ensuring a track has prominence, which usually means getting it included in playlists on the streaming services. The label may also promote the artist to other decision makers and opinion formers within the industry, usually on a more informal basis.

PRESS

A key component of a label marketing campaign is getting media coverage for the artist and their release. The label usually takes responsibility for this activity, either utilising in-house publicity teams or hiring the services of external music PR agencies. Although the label is primarily promoting an artist's new recordings to blogs, websites, magazines and newspapers, it may also promote the artist's other

activity if it believes this will lead to extra coverage which, in turn, further promotes the new record.

PROMOTIONS

In addition to getting media coverage for an artist's release, the label will also seek to get the new music – specifically the single releases – played on radio and TV, and in relevant clubs. Labels usually have separate PR teams working on this - usually referring to as the promotions or plugging team – or again may outsource this work to an external promotions agency.

SOCIAL MEDIA & DIGITAL CHANNELS

Another key component of a label marketing campaign is the use of social media and other digital channels such as email. Most artists will have active social media channels and email lists already, and the label will work with artist and management on creating bespoke content for these channels around the new release. This may also involve the label putting some advertising spend into social media, especially Facebook. The label may also have its own digital channels via which it will promote the release.

SYNC

Beyond generating revenue through the sale and streaming of the artist's recordings, the label may also seek opportunities to have tracks synchronised into TV programmes, movies, adverts and games. This work involves pitching tracks to music supervisors and negotiating deals with potential sync clients.

WHAT DOES YOUR PARTNER WANT?

- [ ] Exclusivity

- [ ] Copyright Ownership

- [ ] Control Of Recordings

- [ ] Majority Cut Of Revenue

- [ ] 50/50 Split Of Revenue

- [ ] Minority Cut Of Revenue

- [ ] Cut Of Other Revenues

Some labels are more proactive than others when it comes to sync, though most will usually be pitching tracks from across its catalogue to potential sync clients, rather than specifically seeking opportunities for any one artist at any one time.

OTHER COMMERCIAL OPPORTUNITIES

The label may also be seeking other commercial opportunities that benefit both it and the artist. This includes exploiting the artist's recordings by placing them on compilation albums and possibly pursuing brand opportunities other than sync. It may also include seeking commercial opportunities beyond the artist's actual recordings if the label is cut into other any of the artist's other revenue streams such as merchandise, brand partnerships and direct-to-fan.

Two: The Deal

All artists need business partners to provide at least some of the services outlined in Section One.

An artist may seek to do an all encompassing deal with a single label that provides all of these things. Or they may seek to engage a number of companies that together provide all of these services.

Or they may seek to do a deal with a label – or a label services company – to provide some of these services, while the artist's management company provides the rest.

WHAT THE LABEL PARTNER WANTS

EXCLUSIVITY

A label partner will usually want some sort of exclusivity arrangement with the artist. In the case of a traditional record deal, this would usually mean that the artist is obliged to deliver a certain number of recordings to the label and is not allowed to make or release recordings with any other parties until that obligation has been met (or the label has decided not to exercise its right to receive additional recordings).

REVENUE SHARE

With a few exceptions, label partners don't usually expect to charge upfront fees to the artist. Rather the label initially provides its services for free and then shares in any revenue the artist's recordings generate. How this revenue is shared varies hugely from deal to deal – in a classic record deal the label keeps the majority of the money, in a modern distribution deal the artist keeps the majority of the money. The label will also likely be able to recoup some or all of its costs before the revenue share arrangement kicks in, either from the total income pool or specifically the artist's share.

> 66 **under a classic record deal the label would own the copyright in any sound recordings generated under the deal. This means that the controls that come with the sound recording copyright belong to the label – not the artist – and therefore it is the label that is empowered to exploit those controls** 99

COPYRIGHT OWNERSHIP

Under a classic record deal the label would own the copyright in any sound recordings generated under the deal. This means that the controls that come with the sound recording copyright belong to the label – not the artist – and therefore it is the label that is empowered to exploit those controls for profit.

Under UK law, if the label arranges for the recordings to be made, it would be the default owner of the copyright anyway. Where the recordings have already been made prior to the label's involvement, those rights would be assigned to the label through contract. The label may own the copyright in the artist's sound recordings for 'life of copyright' – so 70 years after release in the UK – or the label may be the rights owner for a period of time after which the copyright reverts to the artist.

Distributor and distribution deals do not usually involve copyright assignment, though the distributor or label will still often be granted an exclusive licence to exploit the artist's sound recordings for a set period of time, and will likely act as if it was the copyright owner while those deals are still valid.

ANCILLARY REVENUES

Traditionally a record label was only cut into the artist's recorded music revenue stream. Other revenue streams – such as publishing (ie the monetisation of the separate song copyright), live, merchandise, direct-to-fan and brand partnerships – were not part of the deal. Artists would usually enter into deals with other business partners to capitalise on these other revenue streams.

However, as the value of recorded music slumped in the 2000s, many labels started to demand a cut of some of the other revenue streams too, especially with new talent deals. The labels argued that it was their investment and marketing that unlocked these other revenue streams and that, as the financial return on recordings had declined, they needed a share of other

> **❝ artists like to retain ownership of their copyrights, though most new talent deals involve some copyright assignment to the label, and in the case of major label deals that may well be for life of copyright. Artists may be able to negotiate back some of those copyrights in future deals with the label, though that option is not guaranteed ❞**

revenues to justify their upfront commitment.

Which other revenue streams a label might share in, and quite what that means, varies greatly from deal to deal. Labels usually refer to these as 'ancillary revenues', which tells you that most labels are still primarily interested in partnering with artists on their recordings, and involvement in other aspects of the artist's business is seen as secondary, even if those other revenue share arrangements might prove to be as lucrative.

WHAT THE LABEL PARTNER PROVIDES

INVESTMENT
For new artists in particular, the most important aspect of the record deal is the investment the label provides.

The label invests both money – in terms of the cash advance and budgets to pay for external suppliers and advertising – and resources. This investment is secured on future revenues generated by the artist's recordings. In the case of new artists, that can be a risky investment in that the future revenues are not assured. As a result, the label will usually be more demanding in new talent deals.

SERVICES
The label will provide some or all of the services outlined in Section One. The artist's deal needs to outline which services in particular will be provided, with as much clarity as possible as to what the label is committing to the artist in terms of budget, time and expertise. A tricky task for management is then ensuring the label delivers on these

commitments once the deal has been signed.

ROYALTIES

Usually, all monies generated by an artist's recordings will initially go to the label partner, which will then pay the artist their share. The one exception to this is monies generated via the collective licensing system – so when PPL collects in the UK – where 50% of monies will be paid directly to all the performers who appear on any one recording. This is because when the so called 'performing rights' of a sound recording are exploited, statutory Performer Equitable Remuneration is due.

But all other income will be paid to the label partner in first instance. The label partner then needs to pay the artist their share, subject to contract. As mentioned above, the way income is shared between label and artist varies greatly from contract to contract. The label will also likely be able to recoup some or all of its costs before the revenue share arrangement kicks in, either from the total income or specifically the artist's share.

Three: Negotiation Points

An artist's manager and lawyer will usually negotiate the deal with the label partner.

Like any business deal, the negotiations will cover a number of topics, but there are usually four key elements to the deal.

COMMITMENTS

What is the label committing to the artist in terms of investment and services? And what is the artist committing to the label in terms of number of recordings, time and exclusivity? While these commitments will be outlined in contract and therefore in theory enforceable by law, in reality there needs to be a degree of trust between the artist and label with regard each party's willingness and ability to deliver.

COPYRIGHT OWNERSHIP

Who owns the copyright in the sound recordings created under the deal? If the label is the copyright owner, does the artist have any contractual rights over how the recordings are exploited? If the artist is the copyright owner, does the label have an exclusive licence to exploit those rights, and are there any limitations to that licence?

Artists like to retain ownership of their copyrights, though most new talent deals involve some copyright assignment to the label, and in the case of major label deals that may well be for life of copyright. Artists may be able to negotiate back some of those copyrights in future deals with the label, though that option is not guaranteed.

ROYALTIES, RECOUPMENT & DISCOUNTS

The contract will set out how revenues will be shared. Where the label is the copyright owner, it pays the artist a royalty on revenues generated. Where the artist is the copyright owner, the label charges a commission on revenues generated. In many ways the distinction is merely semantic, though these respective deal types are often viewed quite differently.

Either way, the artist will usually receive a percentage of revenues generated. There may be one percentage across the board or the percentages may differ depending on the revenue stream - eg 15% on CD, 20% on stream, 50% on sync. The contract may also provide 'discounts' to the label, so that in certain scenarios – such as if income comes in via a non-UK subsidiary of the label – a lower royalty rate applies.

The contract also needs to define what the percentages specifically apply to – if the artist is due 20%, it needs to be clear "20% of what". The contract may allow the label to make 'deductions' to income – possibly to cover specific identifiable costs or possibly more generic deductions – before the percentage due is calculated, therefore reducing the overall royalty that is paid.

The label will also usually be allowed to recoup some or all of its costs out of the revenue generated before the artist is paid any money at all. The contract needs to set out what costs are recoupable in this way. Also, are these costs recouped out of all the income that comes in or from just the income allocated to the artist? The former arrangement would usually be referred to as a 'profit share deal' while the latter would be referred to as a 'royalties deal'. The 'royalties deal' arrangement is actually more common.

To illustrate the difference, take this example: the artist and label are on a 50/50 split, there are £100K in recoupable costs, and £250K in income has so far been generated. On a profit share arrangement, the first £100K would go to the label, and the next £150K would be split 50/50, so the artist gets £75K. On a royalties arrangement, half of the money would be allocated to the artist – so £125K – of which £100K would be taken to cover the label's recoupable costs, so the artist gets £25K.

Arguably, many contracts have overly complicated systems in place for royalty payments, especially when it comes to discounts and deductions, many of which came about in the physical era and don't make sense in the streaming age. Managers support simpler royalty arrangements – with fewer or no discounts and deductions – and some labels and, especially, distributors, already offer such simpler arrangements.

REPORTING

As most monies generated by the artist's recordings go through the label at first instance, the artist is reliant on the label to report all income, sums received and royalties due to the artist.

The shift to streaming has created a number of challenges in this regard, because with streaming there is so much more data to report. Though at the same time new technologies should also make the crunching and distribution of this data simpler if the right platforms can be built.

The streaming services also provide valuable usage data as well as royalty data which can inform an artist's wider business.

While some streaming services provide this information directly to artists, others only provide data to labels and distributors, so artists rely on their label partners to access this information.

Managers recognise that some labels and distributors have invested heavily in building platforms to more efficiently share royalty and usage data, though there is still much room for improvement here across the industry.

The MMF Transparency Guide goes into all this in more detail, but ensuring the artist has access to this information is something that now needs to be considered when entering into a deal with a label partner.

Four: Deal Types

There is a range of label partners and deal types for artists to choose from.

As mentioned above, some of these label partners are record labels in the traditional sense, while others may call themselves distributors or label services companies. However, all offer at least some of the services described in Section One.

Not all these label partners and deal types are available to all artists. The more risk a label partner needs to take, the more selective they will be in choosing which artists to work with. Quite what partners and deal types are available – and which are most desirable – will often depend on where the artist is in their career, and they will likely work with different

kinds of partners signing different types of deals as their career progresses.

DEAL 01: DIY DISTRIBUTOR – FEE BASED
These companies provide basic digital distribution, getting tracks into most digital platforms (download stores and streaming platforms) and providing usage and royalty data back from the services. These companies don't usually provide proactive marketing services though may provide some digital marketing tools. These services are usually available to all and any artists with a menu of off-the-shelf packages to choose from. They charge the artist a nominal set up fee for each release but then pass on 100% of the income generated. Some DIY distributors

actually provide the basic distribution free of charge and then try to upsell premium services. There is usually only a nominal commitment to these services, meaning artists can cancel contracts by providing only minimal notice.

DEAL 02: DIY DISTRIBUTOR – COMMISSION BASED

These companies also provide basic digital distribution, getting tracks into most digital platforms and providing usage and royalty data back from the services. Likewise, these companies don't usually provide proactive marketing services though may provide some digital marketing tools. The difference with these companies is that instead of charging a set fee, there are no upfront costs and the distributor instead takes a cut of any income generated. These services are usually available to all and any artists, though some might employ some sort of selection process. There is usually only a nominal commitment to these services, meaning artists can cancel contracts by providing only minimal notice.

DEAL 03: DIY DISTRIBUTOR WITH ADVANCE

DIY distributors usually provide artists with the tools to get their music into the digital platforms and then pass on any monies as they are generated. However, some DIY distributors have also started offering advances on future income in some scenarios. Such advances are usually made based on past performance, ie where a distributor can see what income an artist has generated in the last year and can advance money based

on that information. The idea is that by advancing on future income the artist may be able to fund some marketing that, hopefully, will boost streaming and therefore revenue. The terms of this advanced income varies, and usually locks the artist to the distributor until any advance has been paid back.

DEAL 04: DISTRIBUTOR

Artists can also seek to do deals with more conventional music distributors, which traditionally worked for independent labels, but which may now work directly with artists too. There is usually more flexibility in these deals, rather than the distributor offering off-the-shelf packages.

Conventional distributors will likely want a higher commission than a DIY distributor, but should offer more services in return, in particular B2B marketing, helping to get releases stocked by retailers and playlisted by streaming platforms. Most of these distributors can also assist in physical product distribution, either directly or via third parties, where an artist plans a physical release.

Artists can usually negotiate advances from distributors, but again this will primarily be based on past financial performance. The advance will then be recoupable from the artist's share of subsequent income. More conventional music distributors will usually want a longer commitment from the artist than a DIY distributor, ie a contractual commitment that they will work together for a set period of time.

> **❝ the more risk a label partner needs to take, the more selective they will be in choosing which artists to work with ... quite what partners and deal types are available – and which are most desirable – will often depend on where the artist is in their career ❞**

DEAL 05: DISTRIBUTOR WITH MARKETING

Many distributors now offer consumer marketing as part of the deal. Quite what this means varies greatly from distributor to distributor. Some distributors have in-house marketing teams while others will commit to hire external agencies. At least some of the costs associated with this marketing will likely be recoupable.

DEAL 06: DISTRIBUTOR WITH LABEL SERVICES

Some distributors offer a range of other label services in addition to distribution and marketing, ie some of the other services outlined in Section One above. The range of services on offer varies from company to company, and which services are included varies from deal to deal, though most distributors assume that the artist has already recorded the album before engaging their services. Distributors of this kind usually offer a lot of flexibility as to what services are part of the deal, so that artists can pick and choose what they require. The deal obviously needs to set out what costs are recoupable.

DEAL 07: DISTRIBUTION DEAL WITH A LABEL

Many record labels now offer distribution or services deals as well. These may be through separate divisions that are basically distributors as described above, or an artist might be able to sign a distribution deal with a more conventional label. In the latter option, the label may operate more like the label services agency described above. Or the label may actually provide all the services associated with a traditional record deal, but without any copyright assignment. This could be seen as the best of both worlds, though deals of this kind are most commonly offered to more established artists.

DEAL 08: ASSIGNMENT DEAL WITH A LABEL (PROFIT SHARE)

This is a more traditional record deal, in which most of the services outlined in Section One are provided, including a cash advance, and the label is involved in the recording of the album. The copyright in any sound recordings belongs to the label, at least for a time. Under a profit share arrangement, any recoupable costs are recouped out of all the income generated, not just the artist's share. These deals are traditionally offered by smaller independent labels which would generally commit to invest less money upfront. All of the label's costs would commonly be recoupable, and the subsequent split would usually be 50/50.

DEAL 09: ASSIGNMENT DEAL WITH A LABEL (ROYALTY DEAL – INDIE)

This is also a more traditional record deal, in which most of the services outlined in Section One are provided. Indeed, under more conventional record deals of this kind the label may choose to go beyond their contractual commitments in distributing and marketing the release, especially if it feels like the record is gaining momentum. The copyright in any sound recordings belongs to the label, at least for a time.

Under the royalty deal arrangement, it is agreed which of the label's costs are recoupable (this commonly includes the advance, recording costs, videos and TV advertising) and these come out of the artist's share of income. Although indie labels may be more generous on royalty splits than the majors, these deals would usually still see the label keeping the majority of the income generated.

Indie labels generally can't afford to invest as much upfront as a major, but are usually more flexible on copyright assignment for a set term (rather than life of copyright), are less likely to apply complicated discounts and deductions, are less likely to interfere artistically, and are more likely to continue working an album that doesn't enjoy immediate success if they believe it still has potential.

DEAL 10: ASSIGNMENT DEAL WITH A LABEL (ROYALTY DEAL – MAJOR)

This is basically the same as the indie label deal described above. Again, the label provides most of the services described in Section One and may choose to go beyond their contractual commitments in distributing and marketing the release, especially if it feels like the record is gaining momentum. The copyright in any sound recordings belongs to the label, some costs are recoupable out of the artist's share, and the label likely keeps the majority of the income.

Major labels are generally able to invest more money upfront and have access to global infrastructure if the local division can convince divisions in other countries of an artist's international potential. Major labels are more likely to push for assignment for life of copyright and to apply complicated discounts and deductions to income. They may seek to interfere artistically – though this happens a lot less than it used to – and major labels generally expect more immediate results from releases.

WHAT SERVICES DOES EACH DEAL PROVIDE?

	DIY – FEE	DIY – COMM	DIY+ADVANCE	DISTRIBTOR	DISTRIBTOR+M	DISTRIBTOR+S	DISTRIBUTION	PROFIT SHARE	INDIE LABEL	MAJOR LABEL
Cash Advance	✗	✗	✔	✔	✔	✔	✔	✔	✔	✔
Recording Costs	✗	✗	✗	✗	✗	✗	✗	✔	✔	✔
Artist Dvlpmnt	✗	✗	✗	✗	✗	✗	✗	✔	✔	✔
Product Dvlpmnt	✗	✗	✗	✗	✗	✔	✔	✔	✔	✔
Digital Dist	✔	✔	✔	✔	✔	✔	✔	✔	✔	✔
Manufacture?	✗	✗	✗	✗	✗	✔	✔	✔	✔	✔
Physical Dist	✗	✗	✗	✔	✔	✔	✔	✔	✔	✔
Consmer Mktng	✗	✗	✗	✗	✔	✔	✔	✔	✔	✔
B2B Mktng	✗	✗	✗	✔	✔	✔	✔	✔	✔	✔
Press	✗	✗	✗	✗	✔	✔	✔	✔	✔	✔
Promotions	✗	✗	✗	✗	✔	✔	✔	✔	✔	✔
Social & Digital	✗	✗	✗	✗	✔	✔	✔	✔	✔	✔
Sync	✗	✗	✗	✗	✗	✔	✔	✔	✔	✔

Remember – every deal is different. This chart simply provides a guide to the kinds of services the different deal types might commonly provide.

Section Five: Trends & Challenges

Artists have a greater range of label partners and deal types to choose from today than in the past.

Traditional deals remain attractive if an artist seeks a single business partner to take on full control of their recorded music and provide all the services outlined in Section One, but the label will likely seek copyright ownership and royalty rates in its favour.

For artists who – probably with their management – can handle areas like organising recordings and planning marketing campaigns themselves, the various distributor and distribution deal options are attractive, enabling the artist to pick and choose which services they take and – by reducing the label's risk – being able to demand more favourable terms when it comes to copyright ownership and royalties.

This puts more strain onto management, both in terms of navigating the deals on offer, sourcing alternative finance, and in providing some of the services that were previously handled by the label. Though as more artists pursue distributor and distribution deals, managers may find they can negotiate more favourable deals with more conventional labels in an increasingly competitive market place. More optimistic managers also hope that this market pressure might encourage labels to be more transparent and flexible.

However, one key challenge that remains is that, in a recorded music market that continues to evolve rapidly, negotiating future proof deals – ie deals that remain logical and fair as the recorded music business changes – is difficult.

This is principally a problem where deals involve assignment for life of copyright because, while an artist may only be actively working on new content with a label for a few years, they will be receiving royalties from their label partner for at least the next 70 years. And the recorded music industry will likely go through several revolutions in that time, making legacy contract terms impractical and inequitable.

This is proving problematic today with legacy contracts from the Twentieth Century when assignment for life of copyright was the norm. Managers feel that – in the absence of an industry-wide initiative to bring old contracts into the modern age – legislative change is required to empower artists to bring old deals in line with current standards.

APPENDIX TWO:
TRANSPARENCY GUIDE

WELCOME TO THE TRANSPARENCY GUIDE

One of the key issues raised during the 'Dissecting The Digital Dollar' roundtables was the need for more transparency in the digital music market.

To achieve greater transparency, managers need to be clearer about what specific data and information is required for artists to fully understand and capitalise on the potential of the rapidly expanding streaming sector.

This Transparency Guide seeks to do just that, identifying twenty pieces of data and information, and explaining how they fit into the development and growth of each artist's business.

Introduction

During the 'Dissecting The Digital Dollar' roundtable discussions held by the Music Managers Forum in 2016, transparency was repeatedly identified as one of the key issues in the streaming music business today.

The record industry's shift to digital should have made it easier for managers to track and audit how their artists' recordings are performing. However, the opposite has often been the case. In the streaming domain in particular, it has actually become harder to fully track and audit an artist's recordings, and sometimes impossible.

Some of this is simply down to the challenge of shifting to a new business model, where plays rather than sales generate revenue; where income is primarily revenue share based on consumption share; where royalty payments are very small but very frequent; and where unprecedented amounts of data about consumer behaviour are now available.

All the stakeholders in recorded music – including digital service providers (DSPs), record labels, distributors, music publishers, collective management organisations (CMOs), artists, songwriters and managers – are still adjusting to this new business model.

Artists, songwriters and managers need to be clearer about what information they require. Labels, distributors, publishers and CMOs need to invest in and build platforms that aggregate and share this information in a timely and user-friendly way. And the DSPs need to make sure they are collecting and passing on the required data in the first place.

However, some of the transparency issues are the result of corporate culture at the major music companies, and non-disclosure agreements between the DSPs and the labels, distributors, publishers and CMOs. These NDAs often prevent artists and songwriters from being able to properly audit their royalties and to assess the relative commercial merits of different DSPs.

Most people in the recorded music industry agree that there needs to be more transparency: but who needs to be more transparent about what, exactly?

There is an assortment of data and information artists, songwriters and their managers require access to; some of which is already forthcoming, some of which is available in a limited form, and some of which is currently entirely absent.

In order to further inform this side of the digital dollar debate, CMU Insights consulted a number of leading UK artist managers about the kinds of data and information they need to properly inform and audit their clients' artist businesses.

Based on those conversations, this MMF Transparency Guide outlines in some detail the data and information managers need access to. By itemising this data and information in one place, managers can more easily identify what they are currently missing, and more easily assess how different business partners are performing.

Meanwhile labels, distributors, publishers and CMOs can use this information to inform the development of their own data platforms and the evolution of their transparency policies. And where these business partners say the issue is with the DSPs, artists and songwriters can join with the labels, distributors, publishers and CMOs in putting pressure on the digital companies to make the required information available.

One:
Who Should Provide The Data?

In most cases, business partners sit between an artist/songwriter and the DSP – ie a label, distributor, publisher and/or CMO. We will collectively refer to these entities as 'rights partners' in this guide. In the main artists and songwriters rely on these rights partners to provide them with the data and information they require.

That said, some DSPs - most notably Spotify - provide usage data directly to artists and managers. This is a highly valued service and managers would [a] like to see other DSPs follow Spotify's lead and [b] like this DSP-to-artist provision of data to include royalty as well as usage information.

However, even if all the DSPs provided certain kinds of data directly, artists and managers would still primarily rely on their rights partners to access required information. Partly because many key data elements can only be provided by the rights partner. And partly because artists and managers need to compare how their music is performing on different DSPs side-by-side.

To that end, rights partners need to develop (or continue to develop) data and information sharing systems, most likely through an online portal – and preferably one portal for all data – which provides top line summaries, the facility to drill down to specifics, and tools to analyse trends. Larger rights partners will likely build their own systems, while smaller companies will seek to utilise third party technologies.

This requires investment from the artists' rights partners, and managers recognise that this will take time. Though such portals are now a simple

STREAMING SERVICE

COLLECTING SOCIETY

DISTRIBUTOR

MUSIC PUBLISHER

RECORD LABEL

ARTIST & SONGWRITER

In most cases business partners sit between the streaming platform and the artist/songwriter cost of sale for rights partners, and as streaming takes the recorded music industry back into growth now is the time for those partners to invest.

The quality of these data reporting systems will increasingly become a key factor when artists and

songwriters decide which rights partners to work with, and therefore a rights partner which implements best practice transparency policies and builds the best data reporting systems will enjoy competitive advantage as a service provider to music creatives.

Two: Data Types

It is useful to split the information artists and managers require into three groups:

1. Usage Data

2. Royalty Data

3. DSP Deal Information

Artists and managers need each of these for different reasons:

■ Usage Data to inform the artist's wider business and marketing activity.

■ Royalty Data to audit income and enable financial planning.

■ DSP Deal information to audit income and to assess which DSPs an artist should prioritise.

Three: Usage Data

This is the data that relates to how an artist's music is being consumed on the streaming platforms, both track-by-track, and overall.

TRACK PLAYS (BY TRACK)

What? Quite simply, how many times any one track has been played, in any one day, week, month or in total since release. Clarity is required on what constitutes a 'play', ie what portion of a track must be consumed for a play to be counted. Track play information should be shown in total, but also broken down by DSP, country and product type (ie free stream v premium stream) – as each of these

impact on the royalties paid.

Why? This information tells an artist/ manager which tracks are most popular, is a key metric in how streaming royalties are calculated, and can be used to assess the success of marketing activity.

SOURCE OF PLAYS (BY TRACK)

What? For all the plays a track has enjoyed in any one day, week, month or in total since release, how many: were directly requested by the user, were played as part of an album, originated in some kind of personalised radio feed, originated

142

from a user's personal library, or originated from a third-party playlist? Third-party playlists may be operated by the DSP itself, or a label or media partner, or any individual user. Where a playlist is the source of plays, artists and managers need to know which playlists contributed the plays (or, at least, significant numbers of plays).

Why? This information informs marketing activity, and allows artist/manager to know which playlists are most important in driving streams for their music.

SKIP INFO (BY TRACK)

What? How many times a track was skipped, including a breakdown of at what point in the track skips occurred. It is useful to cross reference this information with source of plays, so to see if users who specifically selected a track or album are skipping, or whether the skips are coming from users of personalised radio style services or subscribers to a third-party playlist that has included the artist's track.

Why? This information informs marketing activity in terms of the suitability of third-party playlists for promoting an artist's music, can inform decision making when it comes to single releases and set lists, and could ultimately inform the songwriting process.

PLAYLIST ADDS (BY TRACK)

What? Information on how many publicly accessible playlists currently include an artist's track, which playlists those are, and the subscriber numbers for each playlist. As a

playlist may have a single subscriber (ie just its creator), it would be good to be able to filter out only those playlists above a certain number of subscribers.

Why? This helps with the analysis of peaks and troughs in overall listening, and informs marketing activity in terms of which third-party playlists to be targeting.

LIBRARY ADDS (BY TRACK)

What? Information on how many users have saved a track or album to their personal library (ie they saved the track to their personal songs library, albums library or a personal playlist).

Why? In the streaming domain, persuading fans to save a track to their personal library is arguably now the end game of a music marketing campaign and therefore it is useful to have this information to assess the success of marketing activity.

TOTAL LISTENER NUMBERS WITH DEMOGRAPHICS AND LOCATION

What? Information on how many users have listened to music across an artist's catalogue in any one day, week, month or for all time, with a breakdown by gender, age and location (preferably nearest town/city in addition to country).

Why? This is valuable information for artists who are looking to build a wider business around their fanbase, and can inform other artist activity, most notably touring.

TOTAL FAN NUMBERS WITH DEMOGRAPHICS AND LOCATION

What? Information on how many users are currently 'following' an artist on each DSP, with a breakdown by gender, age and location (preferably nearest town/city in addition to country).

Why? As with total listener data, this is valuable information for artists who are looking to build a wider business around their fanbase, and can inform other artist activity, most notably touring.

Four: Royalty Data

This is the data that relates to how much money was generated by an artist's music and what share of that income will be paid to the artist.

TOTAL INCOME GENERATED (BY TRACK)

What? The total sum of money generated by a track, also available broken down by DSP, country and product type. As streaming royalties are calculated monthly, and per-stream rates may differ from month-to-month, this information cannot be accurately provided any more frequently than monthly. Though estimated income could be calculated based on total number of plays so far this month and an estimated per-stream payment, though the reliability of per-stream estimates will vary.

Why? Artists need to know how much money their tracks generated in order to audit the royalties they receive from their rights partners. Comparing income from different DSPs, countries and product types may also influence an artist's marketing priorities, windowing strategy and other activity.

INCOME TYPE (BY TRACK)

What? Most streaming deals are revenue share arrangements based on monthly consumption share. However minimum guarantees per-play are also routinely included, with the minimum per-play fee paid if it is higher than the amount due under the revenue share arrangement. It would be useful to know whether a royalty amount has been calculated based on revenue share or minimum guarantee.

Why? This information is useful for managers looking at fluctuations in royalties over time, as the nature of payment calculations may be a factor explaining such variation.

ARTIST ROYALTY RATE (BY TRACK)

What? For each line of track income, the artist needs to know what percentage of that money they are due to receive under their deal with their rights partner. This may be the same percentage figure for all tracks and all usage of all tracks, or it may vary from track to track, and from country to country.

Why? Artists need to know what cut of streaming income they are due, so that they can audit their royalties and plan their finances.

ANY DISCOUNTS OR DEDUCTIONS APPLIED (BY TRACK)

What? Under contract, a rights partner may be allowed to apply discounts or deductions to income received before applying the royalty rate and working out what the artist is due. Any discounts or deductions should be clearly highlighted, both in terms of what they relate to (eg packaging, advertising, international) and what impact they have on the monies the artist is due (eg lower royalty rate, fees being deducted).

Why? Artists need a full understanding of how their streaming income is being calculated, and this includes detailed information of any discounts or deductions being applied, so that they can audit their royalties and plan their finances.

SPECIFIC CONTRACT TERMS OR COMPANY POLICES APPLIED

What? The rights partner should identify which specific terms in their contract with the artist provide the royalty rate being used and allow any discounts or deductions being applied. This may involve referencing the date of the relevant contract and the number of the relevant term or terms. Even better would be the ability to link through to or drop down the actual contract terms written out in full.

Why? This would simplify the audit process for artists and managers, and allow managers to more quickly address top line questions about rates, deductions and discounts. It would be particularly valuable for artists with contracts that pre-date streams, so that artists and managers can clearly see and if necessary query assumptions made by the rights partner.

Where a rights partner has made a policy decision on how to apply pre-digital contracts in the streaming domain, this policy decision could also be linked to, helping managers to clarify and if necessary query such policies. This would be particularly useful at the major music companies where there can be confusion even within the label as to exactly what policies are being applied when.

TOTAL MONIES DUE TO ARTIST

What? How much money the artist is due for streams of each track, in total, and broken down by DSP, country and product type.

Why? This tells the artist how much money to expect, which tracks, DSPs and countries are generating the most income, and helps with financial planning.

PAYMENT DATES

What? The date when payment will be made to the artist.

Why? This helps with financial planning, especially if there is going to be significant time lag between reporting and payment.

THE TRANSPARENCY GUIDE

Five: Deal Information

This is the information in relation to the deals done between the digital platforms and the labels, distributors, publishers and CMOs.

REVENUE SHARE ARRANGEMENT

What? Most streaming deals are revenue share arrangements based on monthly consumption share. Each rights partner will have different revenue share arrangements with each DSP. Revenue share percentages may also differ between countries and product types. This information should be available to an artist's manager and accountant.

Why? This information is required by the accountant for purposes of audit, and lets managers advise artists on which partners to work with, including which DSPs they should prioritise in terms of partnerships, marketing and fan communications.

MINIMUM GUARANTEE PER STREAM

What? In addition to the core revenue stream arrangement, many streaming deals also include a minimum guaranteed per-play rate. Each rights partner will have different minimum guarantee arrangements with each DSP. Minimum guarantees may also differ between countries and product types. This information should be available to an artist's manager and accountant.

Why? The information is required by accountants for purposes of audit,

and also informs managers as to the relative benefits of different business partners – possibly even more so as there is generally greater variance in minimum guarantee arrangements between different rights partners than with the top level revenue share splits.

OTHER DEAL BENEFITS

What? A streaming deal may also include other benefits to the rights partner, such as equity, cash advances, advertising inventory, fees and access to fan data. Artists and managers should be informed of these benefits.

Why? Again, managers need to assess the relative benefits of different business partners, and the value of these other benefits might offset lower revenue share or minimum guarantees. Artists may also feel that they have a contractual or moral right to share in some of these other benefits, and clarity on what those benefits are allows an open and informed conversation on how that might work.

'BREAKAGE' DISTRIBUTION

What? In the context of streaming, 'breakage' refers to unallocated advances. Which is to say, when a rights partner is advanced more money than, it turns out, they were actually due in any one time period, but under contract is allowed to bank the surplus. Most rights partners have pledged to share this money pro-rata with their artists. Rights

TRANSPARENCY INDEX

Track Plays
Source Of Play
Skip Information
Playlist Adds
Library Adds
Total Listener Nos
Total Fan Nos
Total Income By Track
Income Type
Artist Royalty Rate
Deductions Or Discounts
Relevant Contract Terms
Total Artist Royalty
Payment Date
Streaming Deal Revenue Share
Streaming Deal Minima
Other Deal Benefits
Breakage Policy & Process
Equity Policy & Process
Additional Data Feeds

The Transparency Index — the 20 pieces of data and information artists should have access to — is designed to help managers assess how transparent each business partner really is, and also to provide labels, distributors, publishers and CMOs with transparency targets to aim for.

partners should provide artists and managers with clear guidance on their breakage polices by DSP, what the total breakage amounts per DSP were for any one time period, how an artist's share of breakage is being calculated, and what monies the artist is therefore due. Record companies which distribute recordings on behalf of other record labels should also be clear on whether breakage is shared with artists on distributed labels.

Why? Managers believe that rights partners have a duty to share this extra income stream with their artists. Where a commitment to do so has been made, managers need to know how this commitment is being implemented, so to audit royalties and aid financial planning.

PROFIT OF EQUITY SALE DISTRIBUTION

What? When some rights partners do their first deals with start-up streaming platforms, they will demand equity in the start-up business, which they will subsequently be able to sell for profit. Most rights partners have committed to share the profits from any equity sales pro-rata with their artists. Rights partners should provide artists and managers with clear guidance on what equity they hold, what monies any equity sales generate, how an artist's share of this is being calculated, and what monies

the artist is therefore due. Record companies that distribute recordings on behalf of other record labels should also be clear on whether the profit of equity is shared with artists on distributed labels.

Why? Firstly, managers need to know when their rights partners have equity interests in DSPs, as this may influence the rights partners' priorities. Secondly, managers believe that their rights partners have a duty to share this extra income stream with their artists. Where a commitment to do so has been made, managers need to know how this commitment is being implemented, so to audit royalties and aid financial planning.

ADDITIONAL DATA FEEDS

What? A rights partner may be given access to DSP data beyond that which has been discussed in this guide. Where that is so, managers should know what kind of data the label is accessing, and where appropriate have access to this extra data.

Why? This data likely relates to the artist's fanbase, which actually belongs to the artist not the rights partner. Therefore, artists should be able to also access this data, so to inform their wider business and marketing activity.

Six: Building A More Transparent Digital Music Ecosystem

1. AUDIT

This guide sets out for the first time, in some detail, the different kinds of data and information artists and managers require.

Alongside the guide, managers can also access the MMF Transparency Index, a simple form that allows them to audit each of the rights partners they work with as to what data and information is being provided. Doing so will identify the gaps each rights partner needs to address to achieve total transparency.

Using the MMF Transparency Index, managers can now feedback to their artists' rights partners in a more organised fashion. For those rights partners already proactively building a more transparent digital music ecosystem, this feedback can inform the ongoing development of those partners' own proprietary portals, or their decision making when buying in third party portals. For less proactive rights partners, this feedback will put pressure on those partners to become more transparent.

MMF will also pool the audits conducted by its members so to provide wider assessments of all the key rights partners operating in the UK. It will then provide feedback to each of those key rights partners, as well as publicly celebrating the most transparent companies and organisations. Where rights partners consistently tell MMF that a specific transparency gap is caused by the DSPs, it will take up that issue with the DSPs directly on behalf of artists and songwriters, and all their rights partners.

2. EDUCATION

Another aim of this guide is to educate managers as to what data and information they should be seeking from their artists' rights partners, and how that data and information could and should be utilised within their clients' artist businesses.

MMF will seek to further educate managers on the value of all the different kinds of data and information available, and provide practical advice on what to do with that data and information, and how to integrate streaming data with other fan data.

Some rights partners have questioned whether managers will really utilise all of the data and information outlined in this guide. It is true that not all managers are, as yet, fully utlising even the streaming data they are already receiving.

However managers, like all the rights partners, are on steep learning curve, and are eager to make ever better use of the data and information available as the streaming market matures. As explained in this guide, all of the data and information outlined above adds value to an artist's business.

149

And given adding value to an artist's wider business is the primary aim of all managers, they are eager to access, understand and utilise all the data and information listed in the MMF Transparency Index.

3. STANDARDS

As the digital music ecosystem becomes more transparent, the next obvious requirement will be reporting standards.

A plethora of DSPs, rights partners and third party providers are now developing their own data portals.

As managers routinely work with a variety of partners and providers across their roster of artists, that inevitably means any one manager will be making use of multiple portals.

This can be challenging. Though that challenge is easier to meet if there is some consistency across the industry as to how data is presented in all portals, and in particular the terminology that is used.

No one wants to stop any one DSP, rights partner or third party provider from innovating, and achieving competitive advantage by presenting data and information in the most user-friendly fashion.

However, some data reporting standards will be needed, and this is a discussion that should begin sooner rather than later, so that any standards can be implemented early on in the development of each data reporting portal.

4. THE MORAL RIGHT TO INFORMATION

As we have noted, while there is generally agreement within the music industry that there needs to be more transparency in the digital music ecosystem, there has been some resistance – especially at the major music companies – to provide some of the data and information outlined in this guide.

Managers believe that artists and songwriters have a moral right to know how their recordings and songs are being exploited by streaming services. Managers also believe that total transparency will help enhance the business partnerships struck up between artists and their rights partners, and in turn ensure a healthier streaming music market for all.

A closer working relationship between artists and rights partners – built on total trust – will also enable the wider music community to collaborate more closely where copyright regimes need to be reformed to meet the challenges of the streaming age.

Managers hope to build a more transparent digital music ecosystem through collaboration with their artists' rights partners. However, given resistance to date, it seems likely that the political community will need to facilitate at least some of the conversations around transparency.

With the draft European Copyright Directive including an article on transparency, based on the principle

> **66 managers believe that artists and songwriters have a moral right to know how their recordings and songs are being exploited by streaming services ... total transparency will also help enhance the business partnerships struck up between artists and their rights partners 99**

artists and songwriters have a moral right to information, now is a good time for governments to be instigating this debate within the European Union.

5. FAIRER DEALS

It seems likely that a truly transparent digital music ecosystem will highlight a number of areas of contention between artists and their rights partners – sometimes relating to specific terms in any one artist's contract, sometimes relating to wider issues about how contract terms have been implemented across a whole company, or the entire industry.

Many managers suspect that this is the main reason the major music companies are resistant to total transparency. But where there is a disagreement about the way artist and/or DSP deals are being implemented, it is healthy that all stakeholders have a full understanding of how things are working, so to allow an informed and frank discussion between managers and their artists' rights partners.

Some of these disagreements will be settled on a case-by-case basis, but where there are industry-wide issues, wider discussions may be necessary. To that end, it is important to remember that, while transparency was a key issue raised during the 'Dissecting The Digital Dollar' roundtables, it wasn't the only issue. But many of the other issues raised – including the need for fairer deals for artists and songwriters – need more transparency first in order to be properly addressed.

Which is to say that building a more transparent digital music ecosystem is actually step one to building a fairer digital music business. Managers are, in their nature, pragmatic, and continue to recognise the important role an artists' rights partners play, as investors, distributors, marketers and content specialists. But where artists continue to be treated unfairly, managers will seek to address those issues, in collaborating with the wider music industry, and possibly again with the support of the political community.

GLOSSARY

ANGLO-AMERICAN REPERTOIRE
The exact definition can vary, though this commonly refers to songs registered with CMOs in the UK, Ireland, US, Canada, Australia and South Africa.

ASSIGNMENT
When ownership of a copyright is transferred from one party to another, often from an artist or songwriter to a label or publisher. Assignment is possible under many though not all copyright systems.

AUTHOR RIGHTS
A term from civil law systems which, from a music perspective, means the rights in songs and compositions as opposed to the rights in recordings.

COLLECTIVE LICENSING
When music rights owners license as one, appointing a collective management organisation to license on their behalf. Collective licensing is often subject to extra regulation to overcome competition law concerns.

COLLECTIVE MANAGEMENT ORGANISATION (CMO)
Organisations that represent rights owners when they license collectively.

CMOs usually represent either publishing rights or recording rights, and may only represent reproduction rights or performing rights.

On the publishing side, CMOs may actually control some elements of the copyrights they represent, rather than simply representing them as an agent for their members.

CMOs are also referred to as collecting societies, performing rights organisations or PROs.

COMPULSORY LICENCE
When copyright law obliges rights owners to provide a licence to a certain group of licensees, thus limiting the rights owners' negotiating power. Rights owners are still due royalties, but these will usually be ultimately set by a copyright tribunal or court. Compulsory licences are usually managed by CMOs.

DIGITAL SERVICE PROVIDER (DSP)

A term used to refer to companies which provide digital music services, including download stores and streaming platforms.

FEATURED ARTIST

The musicians whose name or names any one recording is released under, as opposed to session musicians who are simply credited in the small print. Record labels generally sign record deals with featured artists.

MAKING AVAILABLE RIGHT

The specific copyright control exploited by services that make content available via digital channels in a way where the user "may access it from a place and at a time individually chosen by them". Applies to download platforms and probably at least some streaming services (though there remains some debate about this).

MECHANICAL RIGHTS

How publishers usually refer to their reproduction rights, especially when exploited by labels through the recording and distribution of songs.

MUSIC PUBLISHER

Companies that own and control song copyrights. So called because their original business was to publish books of sheet music.

NEIGHBOURING RIGHTS

This term is used to mean a number of different things. In some civil law systems it refers to the sound recording right, as opposed to the 'author right' which covers songs and compositions.

In the record industry it is now often used to refer specifically to the 'performing rights' element of the sound recording copyright. Or it is sometimes used to specifically refer to the performer equitable remuneration that is paid on performing rights income.

PERFORMER ER

One of the performer rights, 'performer equitable remuneration' is when artists – including featured artists and session musicians – enjoy an automatic right to a share in sound recording revenues.

This is a statutory rather than contractual right, and usually cannot be waived or assigned by contract. Performer ER only applies to certain revenue streams, commonly performing rights income.

PERFORMER RIGHTS

The specific rights of performers over recordings on which they appear that co-exist with the rights of the copyright owner, where the performers are not the copyright owners. Performer rights include controls over the fixation and subsequent exploitation of recordings, and the right to equitable remuneration from certain revenue streams.

PERFORMING RIGHTS

The specific controls that copyright owners enjoy over the public performance and communication of their works.

PUBLISHING RIGHTS

The copyright in songs, or specifically lyrics and compositions.

RECORD COMPANY/ RECORD LABEL

Companies that own and control recording copyrights, and also commonly a key investor in artists, especially new artists.

RECORDING RIGHTS

The copyright in sound recordings.

REPRODUCTION RIGHTS

The specific controls that copyright owners enjoy over the reproduction and distribution of their works.

SPECIAL PURPOSE VEHICLE (SPV)

The name used to refer to the joint ventures that have been struck up between the big publishers and CMOs to license Anglo-American repertoire to digital services, representing both the publisher's reproduction rights and the CMOs' matching performing rights.

SYNC

When film, TV, advert or video game producers 'synchronise' existing songs and/or recordings to moving images.